FAMOUS GUNS
from the
Smithsonian
Collection

Hank Wieand Bowman

New York

Contents

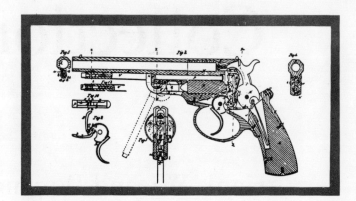

Published 1967 by ARCO PUBLISHING COMPANY, Inc.
219 Park Avenue South, New York, N.Y. 10003

Arco Catalog Number 1606

Printed in the United States of America

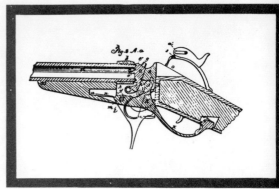

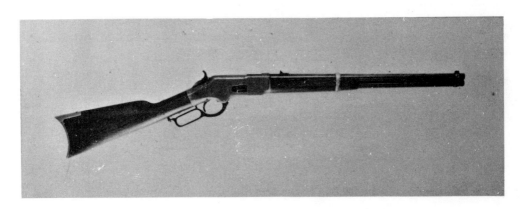

Introduction

Hank Wieand Bowman.

Although it can be said that the field of firearms has never lacked for authors on the subject, the ranks of those who may be classed as top caliber are not swollen. There have been, and are, a very few who really know "The Gun" from every point of view—as collector, as shooting expert, as historian of our past and present. One such, and very high on the list, is the author of the present volume— Hank Wieand Bowman. As an authentic gun expert Hank Bowman has contributed to countless numbers of national magazines, and has written numerous books on the subject.

This last of Hank Bowman's gun books is a fitting number in the sequence that includes FAMOUS GUNS FROM THE WINCHESTER COLLECTION, FAMOUS GUNS FROM THE HAROLDS CLUB COLLECTION, ANTIQUE GUNS FROM THE STAGECOACH COLLECTION. These are the guns that were patented through the years in Washington D.C., the models of which are now in the Smithsonian Institution. All the photographs in this book, unless otherwise credited, are through the courtesy of the Smithsonian. Special thanks are offered to Mr. Edgar M. Howell, and to Mr. Craddock R. Goins, Jr., of the Division of Military History, the Smithsonian Institution.

It is hoped that the present volume will serve not only as a weapon of research for the firearms student, but may also whet the appetite of those who are reading about guns for the first time. In any event, it is sincerely wished that this book, prepared after the untimely death of the author, will serve as a small testimonial of his fine talent, and may induce in the reader the desire to learn more about antique guns, many of which were part of our nation's history.

The Smithsonian Institution.

BACKGROUND OF PATENT LEGISLATION

Numerous and intrepid have been those redoubtable individuals—the inventors—who have braved risks of the market place with the product of their genius. It is the Patent Office that has protected the successful; while in the case of those who failed, it is now sole heir to a unique, if wanting effort. In sum, the U.S. Patent Office is indissolubly linked with the story—one must say the Romance— of the firearm.

THE YEAR 1836 is of vital importance to contemporary firearms collectors and historians. That year a change of laws and a hotel fire materially altered firearms collecting and study.

Aside from a three-year period from 1790 through 1793, during which there is no record to indicate that any firearms or small arms developments were patented, until 1836, inventors were not required to accompany patent applications with a working model of their inventions, but some few elected to do so.

The U.S. Patent Act of 1836 re-established the requirement that an invention, in order to be patentable, must incorporate novelty and usefulness; must not have been invented or used before, and the patent applicant was required to file specifications, drawings and a working model. The requirement for a model continued through 1870 when the Patent Act of July 8th of that year provided that models need only be furnished by special request of the Commissioner of Patents. For another ten years through 1880, patent commissioners continued to request models in many instances, and in most applications of small arms patents.

Since the firearms that will be described herein largely concern those for which patents were issued between the years of 1836 and 1880, and since photographs are of patent models presently displayed at the Museum of History and Technology (Smithsonian Institution), Washington, D.C., or preserved and under the care and supervision of the Division of Military History of the Smithsonian Institution, since our various patent laws and the activities of the Patent Office had a vital effect on encouraging the development of firearms, at least some of the background concerning our American Patent System and the Patent Office should be of considerable interest to collectors.

Were it not for protection offered to inventors, many of the interesting collectors' items would never have been created. Our patent laws offered inventors an opportunity to profit from their ideas. Without patent law protection, improvements in firearms certainly would have come about far more slowly, or perhaps largely would have been curtailed.

United States patent laws offer inventors of novel and useful products an exclusive right to manufacture and sell, or license others to manufacture and sell their inventions for a prescribed period of years. In essence, a patent creates a monopoly, but a monopoly of the type that long has been recognized as healthy and beneficial to the public.

The first patents, although that word to describe the exclusive right was not to be applied to the practice until the 14th century, were awarded hundreds of years before the birth of Christ.

The Achaeans in the ancient Greek city of Sybaris, about 700 B.C., decreed that confectioners and cooks who created a uniquely excellent product should be permitted sole use of the recipe for a period of one year.

Edward II who ruled England from 1327 to 1377 reserved the right to grant what he termed "Letters of Patent" at his discretion. Unfortunately, this practice was abused by monarchs who succeeded Edward. Necessities such as salt and tea were awarded patents, and Sir Walter Raleigh had a real racket going when he was granted a patent to issue tavern licenses.

In 1623, a Statute of Monopolies was adopted in England. The statute, which prohibited monopolies, made an exception as concerned inventors. The statute recognized the value of offering those with creative ideas exclusive rights, so the issuance of Letters of Patents continued, but still at the whim of monarchs or their representatives and the protection offered usually depended upon the influence of the individual patent holder.

In Italy, the Council of Venice in 1474, recognizing the need of offering some form of protection to those "capable of devising and inventing all manner of ingenius contrivances . . .", granted a legal monopoly for ten years. Infringers of "inventive monopolies" were subject to a fine of 100 ducats plus a dunking in the Grand Canal.

At least one patent infringement led to the coinage of a lasting phrase. John Dennis, an early 18th century critic and playwright, was extremely proud of a special sound effects device he invented and used in stage presentations of his tragedy *Appius and Virginia*. In 1711, Dennis, while still rankled by a lampooning his tragedy had received from the pen of Alexander Pope in Pope's *Essay on Criticism,* attended a rival's play and discovered a replica of his device was being used for thunder effects. Dennis leaped to his feet at the height of the artificial storm, screaming "Some bastard has stolen my thunder!"

Many firearms inventors have since felt the same explosive ire when confronted by infringements either purposeful or accidental.

A British firearms patent issued May 15, 1718, to James Puckle of London fre-

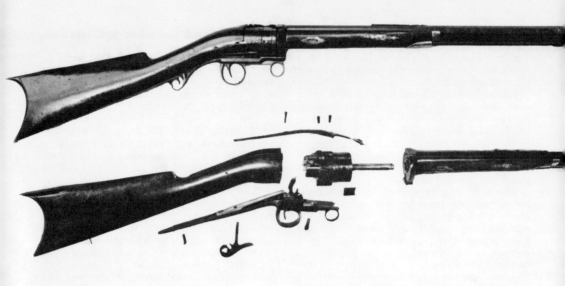

quently has been used as the basis to discount later claims. The Puckle gun, a tripod-mounted affair, had, among other features, a revolving breech and a hand crank to rotate the breech for rapid fire. The Puckle gun appeared to have incorporated elements that closely resembled features later a part of the Gatling and other hand-operated machine guns.

The Puckle patent, called "Defence," was described by its inventor as a "portable gun or machine for defending Yourselves and Protestant causes." It has, over the years, attained considerable fame for an arm that never reached mass production in that its patent drawings illustrated two separate cylinders, one incorporating square chambers and the other round chambers, intended, according to its inventor for "shooting square bullets against Turks . . ." and "for round bullets against Christians."

Patents were not unknown in the North American colonies before the adoption of the Constitution of the United States. A patent for a unique method to manufacture salt was granted by the Massachusetts colony to Samuel Winslow in 1641. Five years later, that same colony's court issued what is thought to be the first American patent on machinery to Joseph Jenkes for a method of manufacturing scythes.

Although patent granting was practiced, there was no consistent set of standards applied to the issuance of patents in the colonies, nor was there any democratic process to insure an inventor that he would

be granted a patent or that once granted, he would have recourse to defend his patent rights. The inventor depended on mercurial political patronage, inconsistently offered by the governing body of his colony or state.

On September 17, 1787, 39 of 42 delegates attending the Constitutional Convention in Philadelphia signed the Constitution of the United States. Included in Article 1, Section 8 was a provision jointly proposed by James Madison, Virginia, and Charles Pinckney, South Carolina, concerning protection for inventors and authors by means of patents. The provision stated: "Congress shall have the power . . . to promote the progress of science and useful arts by securing for limited times to authors and inventors the exclusive right to their respective writings and inventions."

On April 30, 1789, George Washington was inaugurated President of the United States and March 4th, the government under the new Constitution began to serve the people. Washington did not forget Article 1, Section 8 and at a meeting of the First Congress, he urged representatives to give "effectual encouragement to the exertion of skill and genius at home."

The representatives appointed a committee to prepare separate bills on patents and copyrights and on April 1, 1790, President Washington signed the first United States patent bill which recognized the intrinsic right of an inventor to profit from his inventions. No longer need an inventor depend on a special act of a legislature nor,

Two shots of the same Colt, left. The actual patent is nowhere to be found, though it is claimed to be number 9430X, and apparently was destroyed in the Patent Office fire. The weapon is dated Feb. 25, 1836.

Colt's rifle has a revolving cylinder, is octagonal, 31 inch barrel, with rib underneath. It is caliber .30, 50 inches overall length, has a short walnut stock with iron trimmings. The cylinder has 10 chambers, with 1¾" nipples set in end. And—the Colonel himself, with his most famous product, the handgun of course. The famed Paterson revolver is a single-action, octagonal, rifled 8¾" barrel, caliber .36, and 14" overall length. It is 6-chambered, has a revolving cylinder, folding trigger, percussion cap nipples set straight in recesses in the end of the cylinder, and with iron mountings marked on the barrel.

9

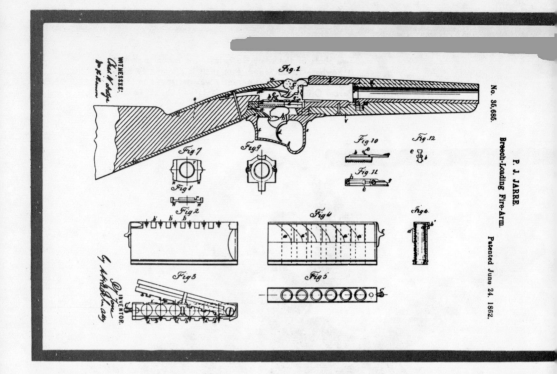

WITNESSES:

INVENTOR.

P. J. JARRE.
Breech-Loading Fire-Arm.

No. 35,686.

Patented June 24, 1862.

in theory at least, would he be required to have political influence in order to gain protection.

Initially, the inventor's application for a patent required that he present specifications, drawings and, if possible, a model.

A board made up of the Secretary of State, Secretary of War and Attorney General were given power to issue patents and to fix the duration of the patent for a period not to exceed fourteen years.

There was a weakness in the new law. The board's authority was absolute. No right of appeal was offered the inventor, but still the arrangement was more equitable than any patent law under any other government.

Thomas Jefferson, as Secretary of the Department of State, became the first supervisor of patents and as such the initial patent examiner. Jefferson was enthusiastic, and according to records, personally examined all applications that came before his board. Fortunately, he was brilliant and had an excellent educational foundation for judgment including a firm background in architecture, astronomy, languages and mathematics. Jefferson, despite an inventive bent, applied for no patents though he is credited with inventing a combination folding chair and walking stick, a revolv-

ing chair and a pedometer. The examiner, too, kept his board posted concerning new scientific developments in Europe. It was Jefferson who first gave members of Congress a detailed report concerning James Watts' steam engine invention.

During the first three years of operation, Jefferson and his board issued 55 patents, none of which concerned mechanical features of firearms.

During 1792 and the early part of 1793, a growing rivalry between the Secretary of the Treasury, Alexander Hamilton and Thomas Jefferson occupied more and more of Jefferson's time and weakened his function as head of the Patent Board.

On February 21, 1793, despite opposition by Jefferson, patent laws were materially changed, the Patent Board was abolished and the examination system was dropped in favor of a simple registration system.

Payment of an application fee of $30 replaced the former far more modest fees of $4 to $5. No requirement existed for an invention to incorporate novelty, usefulness, nor was the patent claimant required to supply drawings or a model. Patent issuance became strictly a clerical matter of paying a fee and without examination, being awarded a patent. The intent of pat-

The repeating firearm of J. Jarre, of Paris, France, was patented June 24, 1862, with the patent number 35,685. The weapon is caliber .58, 32" round smoothbore barrel, and it is 51" overall length. The 5-chambered cylinder slides through the frame from left to right.

At right is the man whose name became indeed an Institution. James Smithson was a British chemist, and he founded the Smithsonian, famed now all over the world. His dates are 1765-1829. Recently, the Smithsonian has expanded to new, very modern quarters in Washington.

Brown Brothers

ent awarding was lost as the function became simply a means to provide added Federal revenue.

Supervision remained under the Secretary of State, but Jefferson resigned due to a conflict of political policy with Washington who had leaned more and more on Hamilton for advice on foreign policy.

Edmund Randolph, aide-de-camp to General Washington during the Revolution, succeeded Jefferson in Washington's cabinet. During Randolph's period of supervision of the Patent Office, Eli Whitney was issued his patent for the cotton gin, a patent that was to have a tremendous economic influence, but one which never proved profitable to its inventor who spent more money in litigation than he netted in sales and royalties. Whitney later was to become a successful contractor for government muskets and was to apply his inventive genius to the development of machinery permitting finishing of identical and interchangeable firearm parts.

When Thomas Jefferson was elected President in 1801 to succeed John Adams, he appointed James Madison, co-proposer of the Constitution's original patent provision, as his Secretary of State. Madison appointed the Patent Office's first salaried chief, Dr. William Thornton, noted for his design of the original plans for the Capitol in Washington.

Thornton was accused of profiting by the office far beyond his $1500 a year salary since he awarded several patents to himself (a practice later prohibited to any Patent Office employee), and was financially associated with John Fitch and his steamboat developments. However, Thornton is credited with successfully persuading the British not to burn the Patent Office, then located in Blodgett's Hotel in Washington, D.C., on E Street, convincing the British Commander that to destroy the contents of the Patent Office would destroy records of value to all mankind.

Dr. Thornton, the first superintendent of the Patent Office, died in 1828. Four additional superintendents served in that post following Thornton's death through to 1836. During that period, the Patent Office continued to function ineffectually not due to personnel involved, but rather to the laws under which the office operated.

John Ruggles, a newly appointed senator from Maine, in 1835 asked the Senate to appoint a committee to study the Patent Office and its laws and was appointed chairman of the committee. Ruggles made public his committee's report on April 28, 1836, and pulled no punches when, among

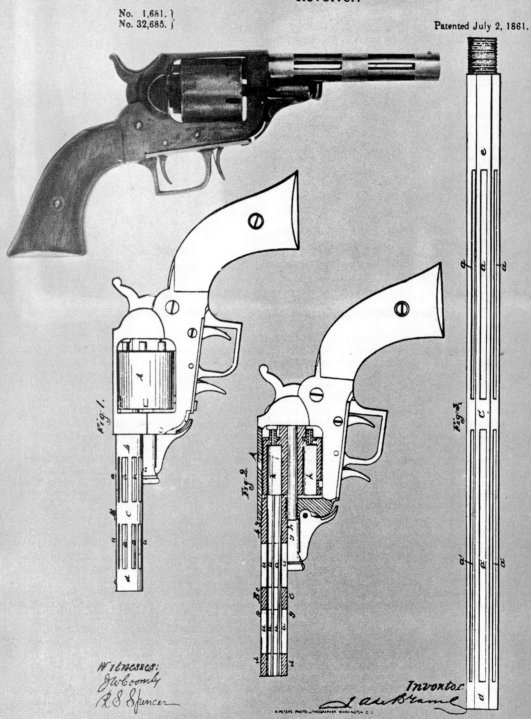

J. A. DeBRAME.
Revolver.

No. 1,681.
No. 32,685.

Patented July 2, 1861.

Witnesses:
J W Coomly
R S Spencer

Inventor:
J de Brame

Patent number 32,685 was taken out on July 2, 1861, by J. A. DeBrame for a 5-chambered revolver with 4" barrel and 9" iron frame. The weapon is .33 caliber. It will be noted that the barrel is slotted. The inventor claimed that following experiments with a whole barrel and with a slotted one, he found the latter preferable because the bullet would be projected with far greater force and with equal accuracy. Mr. DeBrame maintained further that this resulted partly from the prevention of a "less pressure of gas" occuring within the barrel behind the projectile as compared with the pressure of air in front before it left the barrel, and partly from the reduction of friction between the ball and the bore.

other statements, he said, "For more than forty years, the Department of State has passed on every application for patent without any examination of the merit or novelty of the invention. Many of the patents granted are worthless and void. Many are in conflict with one another, and a great many lawsuits arise from this condition.

"Frauds develop, people copy existing patents, make slight changes and are granted patents. Patents have become of little value and the object of the patent laws is in great measure defeated."

Through the efforts of Ruggles and his committee, the Patent Act of July 4, 1836, remedied many of the weaknesses then existing in our Patent System. Once again, patent searches were made to be sure that no "prior art," that is, previous invention or use preceded the patent application.

Even as Ruggles' committee was studying shortcomings of the Patent Office, Letters of Patent were awarded leading to possible conflict of interest. One of these concerned the Samuel Colt patent awarded February 25, 1836, and a possible conflicting patent granted Benjamin and Barton Darling of Bellingham, Massachusetts, presumed to have been dated April 13, 1836. Both were for rotary cylinder pistols.

Seemingly, there are always those who would like to kill and tan the hide of sacred cows. Since Colt firearms have become the established pet of a large segment of collectors, the name Colt for the non-Colt fancier often has become a sacred cow and a target for suspicion and deprecation.

Just as there are literary critics and historians who still argue that Shakespeare's plays were in fact not the work of Shakespeare at all, but of some lesser known writer, there are those who insist that Colt was a mere imitator, that he had little claim to creation of a firearm with a mechanically turned cylinder. Some insist the real inventor was Benjamin M. Darling

who outlived Samuel Colt by some thirty years and who, in later years, declared that he, not Colt, was the creator of the first American revolver.

Some firearms historians have insisted that Colt's prior claim to a multi-shot pistol, with many-chambered breech that revolved by the act of cocking the hammer, forced the Darlings out of business. Since the Darling and Darling-type pepperboxes were made in extremely limited quantity with an estimated maximum production figure ranging somewhere between 100 and 200, it is doubtful that this minimal production would have concerned Colt. Colt, at the time of the Darlings' production, was having too many promotional and sales problems to have initiated legal pressures to put the Darlings out of business for their pepperbox-type "rotary pistols" were not produced after 1840. Though the pepperbox handarms were to become far more popular than Colt's revolving cylinder single barrel revolvers, it was not the Darling-type, but the European-made and American-built pepperboxes of other manufacturers that caused Colt concern. No documents have ever been found to indicate that Colt or his associates initiated or threatened litigation against the Darlings.

One factor that has given the Darling supporters their greatest basis for argument is lack of factual evidence to silence them. There are no Letters of Patent or other specifications and descriptions of claims because on December 15, 1836, there was a disastrous fire in Blodgett's Hotel which still served as the Patent Office. The famous old building which, at one time, had housed the first theater in Washington, was the meeting place for Congress while the Capitol building was being restored after it had been burned by the British in 1814, and which in 1829, had been expanded to include both Patent Office and Washington, D.C. Post Office was completely destroyed. An estimated 7000 patent models, 9000 drawings, 230 books, and all records of patent applications and grants were burned or otherwise ruined. Although Congress appropriated $100,000 to replace the records and many of the valuable and interesting patent models, much of this restoration was dependent upon cooperation of patent holders whose government data had been destroyed.

Neither Darling brother petitioned for a re-issue of his patent though presumably these Letters of Patent were to apply until 1850.

No patent model of a Darling has been located, so if there had been one, it may be

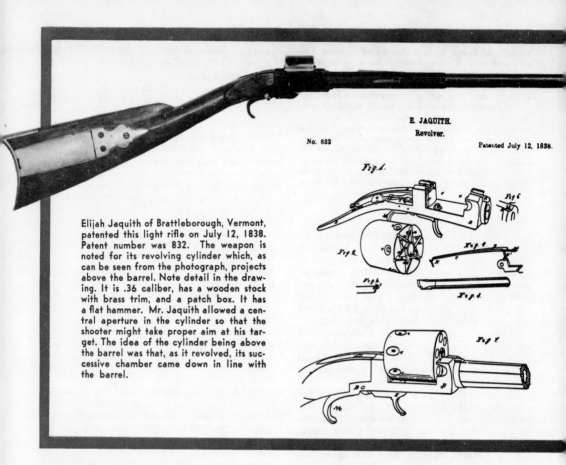

E. JAQUITH.
Revolver.

No. 832

Patented July 12, 1838.

Elijah Jaquith of Brattleborough, Vermont, patented this light rifle on July 12, 1838. Patent number was 832. The weapon is noted for its revolving cylinder which, as can be seen from the photograph, projects above the barrel. Note detail in the drawing. It is .36 caliber, has a wooden stock with brass trim, and a patch box. It has a flat hammer. Mr. Jaquith allowed a central aperture in the cylinder so that the shooter might take proper aim at his target. The idea of the cylinder being above the barrel was that, as it revolved, its successive chamber came down in line with the barrel.

presumed to have been destroyed in the 1836 fire as may have been the original Colt patent model.

Uncontestable facts are that Colt's Letters of Patent predated Darling's patent by approximately six weeks. A day would have been enough. Darlings ceased manufacture of their pepperbox sometime before 1840. Because of markings found on Darling-type pepperboxes owned by various collectors, it can be reasonably assumed that other gunsmiths of the period produced Darling-type pepperboxes with or without Darling consent since brass frame and brass cylinder Darling-types exist marked variously "TEH," "AIS," "ACS" and "J. Engh."

By hindsight, Benjamin Darling doubtless felt he and his brother had muffed a great opportunity, but though their pepperboxes are valued collectors' items today due to their rarity, the brothers Darling, as the holders of the first recorded American pepperbox patent, failed to capitalize on their opportunity and permitted Ethan Allen and others to dominate the lucrative

period of pepperbox sales which from 1840 for nearly two decades outstripped single-barrel revolver sales by far.

In fact, Colt seemingly was far more concerned with the repeater rifle phase of his business than with the handarms and may never have presented a working model of his early handarm to the Patent Office.

The Colt patent handgun model in the Smithsonian collection is certainly not one of the original models or specimen pistols made by Anson Chase of Hartford, Connecticut, or his assistant, William H. Rowe, for the original patent described a shield covering the caps, and this feature was claimed by Colt in his original Letters of Patent "as a security against moisture and the action of smoke upon the works of the lock" and it is featured only in the patent model rifle.

As Colt was later to explain, this feature (the shield) actually caused a chain-fire reaction and when on October 24, 1848, under Re-issue #124, Colt reiterated his specifications, this cylinder cover was eliminated in his claims.

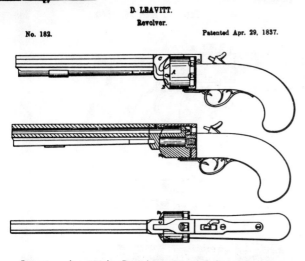

D. LEAVITT.
Revolver.

No. 182.

Patented Apr. 29, 1837.

Patent number 182 by Daniel Leavitt, of Cabotsville, Massachusetts, was for a revolving pistol; April 29, 1837. The barrel is octagonal, 9½ inches in length; caliber .36, and the overall length of the arm is 17½ inches. It has a wooden handle, brass trigger guard, is 7-chambered with a revolving cylinder, the forward end of which is sloped. Percussion cap nipples are on the rear end.

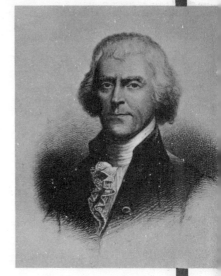

Thomas Jefferson, as Secretary of the Department of State, became the first supervisor of patents.

Colt's initial claims, as listed in the Letters of Patent dated February 25, 1836, were for the following items:

1. "The application of caps to the end of the cylinders.
2. "The application of a partition between the caps.
3. "The application of a shield over the caps as a security against moisture and the action of the smoke upon the works of the lock.
4. "The principle of the connecting rod between the hammer and the trigger.
5. "The application of the shackle to connect the cylinder with the ratchet.
6. "The principle of locking and turning the cylinder.
7. "The principle of uniting the barrel with the cylinder by means of the arbor running through the plate and the projection under the barrel.
8. "The principle of the adopter and the application of the lever, neither of which is used in pistols."

The Hartford, Connecticut-born inventor was certainly not given to modesty, but Colt made no claim to the creation of the first multi-fire rotating cylinder type of firearm. The following excerpts from a speech made by Colt in London at a meeting of the Institution of Civil Engineers in 1851 indicate Colt was quite willing to acknowledge prior use of rotating chambered-breech guns to others, though in typical Colt hyper-sales manner, he couldn't resist pointing out the flaws of each mechanism in turn.

Colt stated in that speech, later published in pamphlet format, that he had been aware ". . . since the year 1835, of the existence of ancient examples of repeating firearms, but it had only been on the occasion of my present visit to Europe in 1851 that I had been able to devote any attention to their chronological history as exhibited in the specimens existing in the museums and private collections to which I have recently gained access."

Colt then went on to describe a 15th century revolving-breech, four-chambered matchlock gun in the Armoury of the Tower of London. He made mention of

15

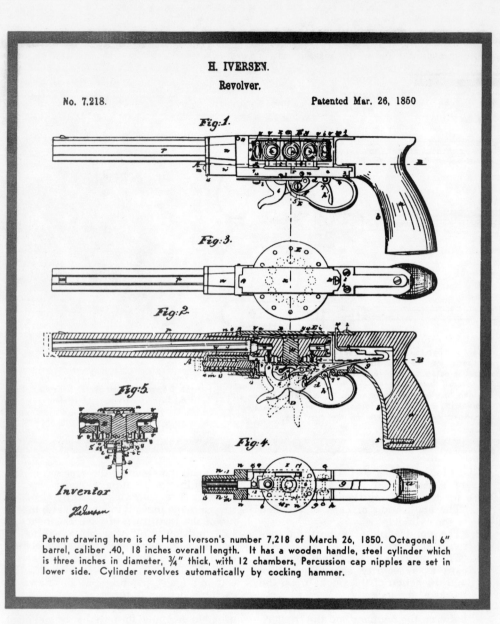

H. IVERSEN.
Revolver.

No. 7,218.

Patented Mar. 26, 1850

Fig:1.

Fig:3.

Fig:2.

Fig:5.

Fig:4.

Inventor

Iverson

Patent drawing here is of Hans Iverson's number 7,218 of March 26, 1850. Octagonal 6″ barrel, caliber .40, 18 inches overall length. It has a wooden handle, steel cylinder which is three inches in diameter, ¾″ thick, with 12 chambers, Percussion cap nipples are set in lower side. Cylinder revolves automatically by cocking hammer.

notches in a flange at the forward end of the breech to receive the end of a spring fixed to the stock for the purpose of indexing each of the four chambers in turn, so as to line up with the barrel. He also referred to two revolving-breech matchlock guns at the Musée d'Artillerie in Paris. Each of these had eight chambers. He described other matchlock arms; a six-chambered revolving-breech wheel lock at the Tower of London, an eight-chambered wheel lock of 17th century vintage in the Hotel Cluny in Paris.

Colt did not mention a prior United States patent, however, although he did refer to Elisha Collier's English patent of August, 1818. Colt mentioned that the arrangement of the flintlock chambered breech firearm had been contrived by Wheeler of Boston, but failed to mention that, although the actual patent records had been destroyed, a partial list of U.S. firearms magazine gun patents from 1802 through 1836 had survived and among them was notation of an invention of a gun that discharged seven or more times, patented

June 10, 1818, by, it appears, A. Wheeler.

Colt, in commenting on the Wheeler design, Collier-patented and English-built revolver, had this to say: "It is not a little surprising that the next example (referring to the Collier flintlock arm) should exhibit nearly all the serious defects which had doubtless been discovered and had been to some extent remedied by the early makers. The objectionable parts of this arm are the priming magazine, the flue, which would conduct the fire round through the different touch holes, and the cap in front, which would direct the lateral fire into the adjoining chambers. The breech is made to bear against the barrel by means of a coiled spring which would probably be efficient while the gun was cleaned, and each chamber is recessed to receive the abutting end of the barrel with the intention of affecting a closer junction. . ."

Colt acknowledged, too, the revolving-breech firearm patented by Londoner Henry Nock in 1787 to which was later applied one of Rev. Forsyth's famous scent bottle-type fulminate ignition systems.

In referring to the possibility of intercommunication of fire from percussion cap in a cylinder revolver, Colt stated ". . . when I enclosed the rear and the mouths of the rotating chambers, the fire, being confined beneath the shield and the cap, was communicated successively to others of the percussion caps, and in front was conveyed into the chambers so that premature and simultaneous explosions of charges necessarily took place."

He further stated, "In consequence of these premature explosions, it became necessary to remove the shield, from over the base of the chamber, and to introduce partitions, between the nipples, or cones, to prevent the fire from spreading to and exploding the adjoining caps; but this only partially accomplished the object."

Colt went on to explain that, despite this modification, during an American government trial of his arms, an accident occurred due to the simultaneous explosion of two chambers. To correct this, he cham-

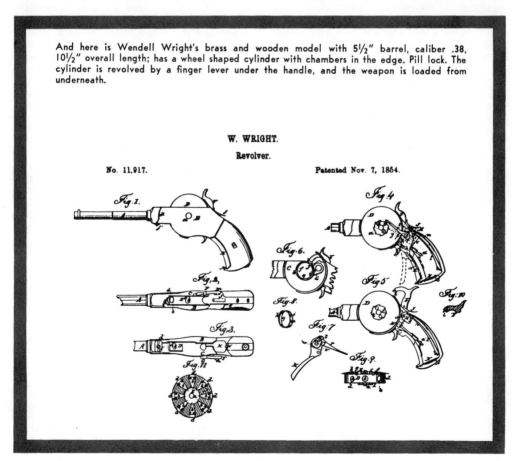

And here is Wendell Wright's brass and wooden model with 5½" barrel, caliber .38, 10½" overall length; has a wheel shaped cylinder with chambers in the edge. Pill lock. The cylinder is revolved by a finger lever under the handle, and the weapon is loaded from underneath.

W. WRIGHT.

Revolver.

No. 11,917.   Patented Nov. 7, 1854.

fered or beveled each chamber "so as to reflect, or throw off at an outward angle, the fire which expanded laterally across their (the chambers) mouths."

He explained that the reason for the alteration was, "that when the lateral fire met the rectangular edge of the orifice of the chambers, the angle of incidence being equal to the angle of deflection, the fire was conducted downwards, or inwards to the charge; but when the flame struck the chamfered edge, the flame was directed outward away from the charge. Unimportant as this alteration may appear, it is proved to be effectual so that if loose powder is placed over the charge in the adjoining chambers, it is not now ignited when the pistol is discharged."

When Colt admitted that he had experienced problems with chain-fire reaction and explained how he had overcome this problem, he failed to mention that Daniel Leavitt may have provided Colt with the answer in Leavitt's Patent #182 of April 29, 1837.

In his claim for a patent in which he, incidentally, disclaimed any novelty as concerned the revolving cylinder, Leavitt specified only one feature, ". . . the giving to the chambered or forward end of the cylinder a convex form, by which the ignition charge in a chamber contiguous to that which is being fired is prevented. . ."

Firearms designers have always been an extremely imaginative group. With the development of percussion ignition, the creative spark of gun inventors burst into a hot flame.

No longer was it necessary to protect loose powder from spilling from primer pans, or depend upon an unwieldy flint for uncertain ignition.

Fulminate salts were destined to provide the key to unlock an entire progression of new developments from percussion cap to self-contained metal cartridge. From the first use of the percussion method of Rev. Forsyth through to present-day automatic weapons, the primer detonated by impact has been used; first in the form of loose fulminate salts, then pills, pellets, caps, tape, disk, cup and other varying types of self-contained cartridges. Within a decade of Scottish minister, Alexander John Forsyth's British patent in 1807 for a firearm lock mechanism using a mixture of fulminate of mercury and potassium chlorate, flint ignition was to be largely abandoned in favor of the newer ignition systems impervious to the effect of weather.

The hot focus of inventors' interest was on faster and simpler means to load and to create increased fire power so that the shooter was not required to carry several arms in order to shoot several times without reloading. Inventive fancy was largely directed toward breech loading and multifire weapons which make up the bulk of the patent models in the Smithsonian collection. Neither breech loading or multifire, of course, was new. Multiple or clusters of barrels, fixed or revolving; superposed charges in single barrels with multiple lock mechanisms; rotating cylinders; magazines of varying types had all been tried before, some with reasonable success considering the limitations of the pre-percussion ignition systems.

Unfortunately, several dozen of the earliest patented firearms are not represented among existing patent models. An H. Rogers, for example, on May 7, 1829, was awarded a patent for a four-barrel revolving gun with percussion lock. If there had been a model of Rogers' gun, it must have been among those consumed by fire in 1836, for no record of such a gun exists at the Smithsonian. Whether Rogers' firearm patent applied to a pepperbox design or to a single barrel arm with revolving cylinder, is not known, but it could be presumed to be the latter, since a Henry Rogers of Middletown, Ohio, is known to have advertised for sale superposed percussion rifles and percussion revolvers between 1828 and 1839.

There is no argument that prior to Ruggles' committee's investigation of the Patent System and Patent Office procedures, there was a lamentable laxity in patent search and patent granting.

Facsimiles of Colt's original patent of February 25, 1836, refer to it as Patent #138. When Colt's 1836 patent was reissued in 1848, the description of its reissuance reads as follows: "Specification forming part of Letters of Patent No. 138, dated February 25, 1836; Re-issuance #124 dated October 24, 1848." The Patent Office seemingly had no logical reason for assigning to Colt Patent #138 on February 25, 1836. If one writes to the U.S. Department of Commerce, Patent Office, Wash-

At right a unique contribution to the development of firearms is Henry S. Josselyn's chain pistol. It was patented on January 23, 1866, number 52,248. The barrel is octagonal and is 4½ inches long. Overall length, though is 9¼ inches. There are 20 chambers 11/16″ in length, and they are fastened together in what might appear to be an endless chain which hangs from a revolving ratchet operated by a lock that brings each chamber under the hammer in turn. This weapon was eventually adapted to use the metallic cartridge. The axis upon which the chain of cartridges rotated was parallel with the bore of the barrel.

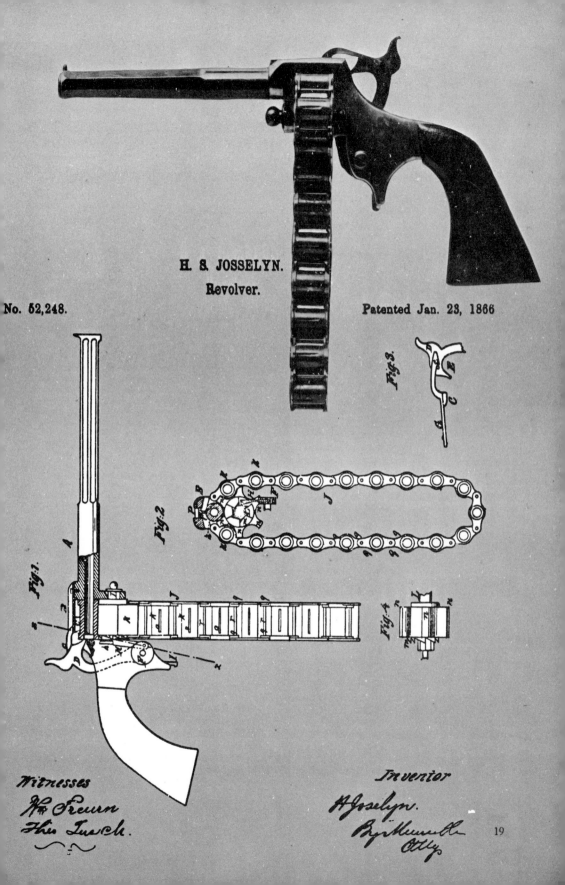

H. S. JOSSELYN.
Revolver.

No. 52,248.

Patented Jan. 23, 1866

Witnesses

Inventor

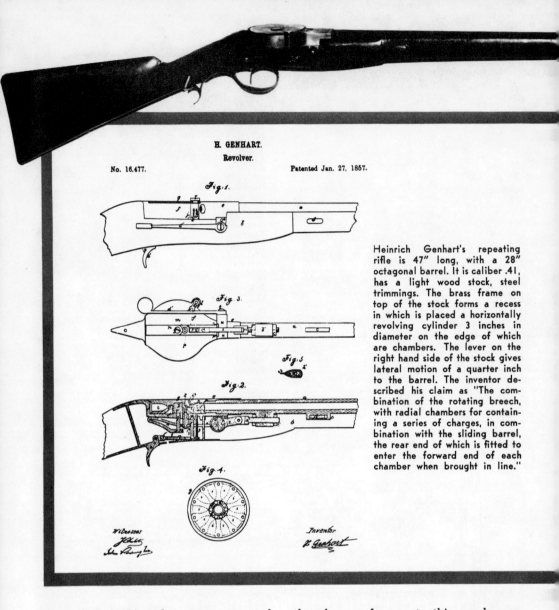

H. GENHART.
Revolver.

No. 16,477.

Patented Jan. 27, 1857.

Fig.1

Fig.3

Fig.5

Fig.2

Fig.4

Heinrich Genhart's repeating rifle is 47" long, with a 28" octagonal barrel. It is caliber .41, has a light wood stock, steel trimmings. The brass frame on top of the stock forms a recess in which is placed a horizontally revolving cylinder 3 inches in diameter on the edge of which are chambers. The lever on the right hand side of the stock gives lateral motion of a quarter inch to the barrel. The inventor described his claim as "The combination of the rotating breech, with radial chambers for containing a series of charges, in combination with the sliding barrel, the rear end of which is fitted to enter the forward end of each chamber when brought in line."

ington, D.C. 20231, and requests a copy of Patent #138 (for which facsimiles of drawings and specifications are available at 50¢ each at this writing, although prior to October, 1965, copies of patent papers cost 25¢), one will receive a drawing and specifications covering a Patent #138 issued to Barnabas S. Gillespie of New York City. This covered an improvement in ice breaking machinery intended to aid in keeping frozen waters open to navigation during the winter season.

It is possible that at some time evidence will be uncovered to explain why the original Colt patent is referred to as #138,

though no reference to this number appears at the Patent Office as concerns anyone except Gillespie. The confusion does serve to indicate that, despite a shake-up and an improvement in patent procedures in 1836 laxity still existed about the middle of the 19th century.

The number of patents, that will be referred to elsewhere as a convenience to firearms students who may want to obtain a complete set of patents for their research files, are based on a chronological numbering system that dates from July 4, 1836, when the Ruggles or the 1836 Patent Act was passed.

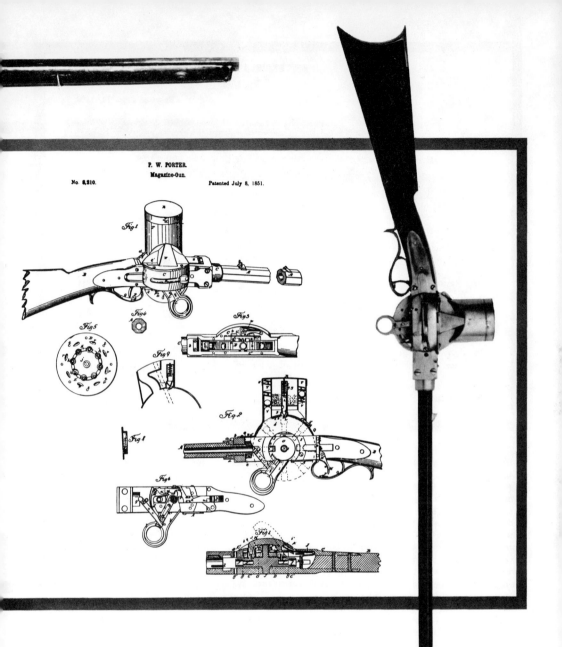

P. W. PORTER.
Magazine-Gun.

No. 8,210.

Patented July 8, 1851.

Mr. Parry W. Porter of Memphis, Tennessee, was the author of the unique weapon above, which is also on our cover. Under patent number 8,210, dated July 8, 1851, the model was filed with the Patent Office. The arm has an octagonal, rifled 28" barrel; is caliber .35, 50 inches in overall length, has a walnut stock, brass trimmings, a steel lock-frame carrying in its center the perpendicularly revolving cylinder which is 4" in diameter, with percussion cap nipples; side hammer. The metal box above the revolving cylinder is $2\frac{1}{2}$" in diameter and 3" high. It forms the magazine for powder and bullets which are fed into the barrel by operation of a finger lever. Open sights are set off to the left of the barrel and a section of magazine is cut away on that side. The stock is broken off just behind the magazine.

BUTTERFIELD & MARSHALL.
Gun-Lock.

No. 24,372.

Patented June 14, 1859.

Drawing shows details of self-priming gun lock patented by Jesse S. Butterfield and Simeon Marshall, June 14, 1859. Magazine below lock forms a receptacle in which primer wafers are carried and are fed forward by cocking hammer. Restoration by R. Klinger.

As a curious sidelight of that act, John Ruggles who fostered the bill, was awarded United States Patent #1 concerning an improvement in tractor power of locomotive steam engines. All U.S. patents are numbered consecutively beginning with the Ruggles patent. Those previously issued have no official number designation.

Another provision of the 1836 Patent Act was that the patent period of "monopoly" continued to be for a period of fourteen years, but subject to extension of seven additional years. In 1839, another important provision was added to our patent laws permitting an American inventor to use publicly or sell his article for two years before applying for a patent without forfeiting his right for a patent.

The 14-year original patent period, plus the possible extension of seven years, continued to be applied until 1861 when the term for a patent grant was changed to 17 years as a compromise between those who favored retaining a 14-year patent period plus an extension, and those who favored abolishment of any extensions.

That same year, the Constitution of the Confederate States of America provided for the establishment of a Patent Office located in the Mechanics Building in Richmond, Virginia. The first Confederate States patent was issued to James H. Van Hauten of Savannah, Georgia, August 1, 1861, for a breech loading gun. Approximately one third of the 266 patents issued by the Confederacy were for firearms and other implements and machinery of war. The final Confederate Patent #266 applied to a percussion cap rammer and was issued to W. N. Smith of Richmond, Virginia, January 6, 1865.

Oddly, during World War II in 1942, the bulk of the U.S. Patent Office was moved to Richmond, Virginia, where it was located for the next five years.

Texas, which dissolved its ties with Mexico and became an independent Republic in 1836, under its Constitution gave its Congress power to grant patents to inventors. The Republic of Texas issued patents until it came into the Union in 1845. Members of Congress urged that former Republic of Texas patents be validated and later similar urging was to be applied to Confederate States patents. In neither instance was congressional action taken, and firearms patents issued by the Republic of Texas and the Confederate States of Amer-

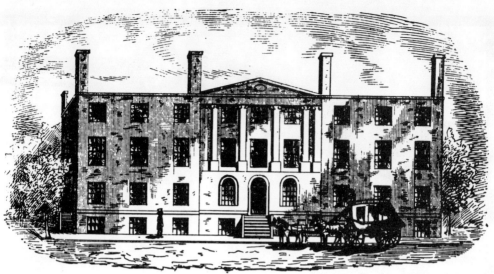

Blodgett's Hotel in Washington, D.C., on E Street, the first home of the Patent Office. It was built in 1793, and burned in 1836. With it went many patent filings and gun models.

ica were never validated by the United States.

Students of firearm history should view with certain skepticism patent dates stamped or engraved on firearms. The fact that an entire firearm is included among patent models at the Smithsonian, or that a patent date is legible on a firearm, is no indication that the patent issued applies to the entire mechanism. Rather it may apply only to those features claimed in the patent letters of specification.

An example of this is the Wesson, Stephens & Miller revolver sometimes erroneously referred to as the Wesson & Leavitt. This single-action, .40 caliber, 6-shot, hand-turned cylinder revolver is marked "LEAVITT'S PATENT . . ." referring to Patent #182 of April 29, 1837. The solid frame tip-up action revolver incorporates only one patented feature awarded Leavitt; that of the convex shape of the forward end of the cylinder and the elliptical shape of the forward end of the chambers.

The Wesson & Leavitts, which were made by the Massachusetts Arms Co. of Chicopee Falls, have mechanically, rather than hand-turned, cylinders and their date of manufacture was from 1849 to 1851. These later arms were found to be an infringement of Colt patents and the company was forced to cease manufacture.

Leavitt's 1837 patent, however, was practical as a solution to prevent accidental ignition of chambers other than the one being purposefully fired, though its de-

Dr. William Thornton (1755-1828), first superintendent of Patent Office, was accused of profiteering, but persuaded British not to burn Patent Office in War of 1812.

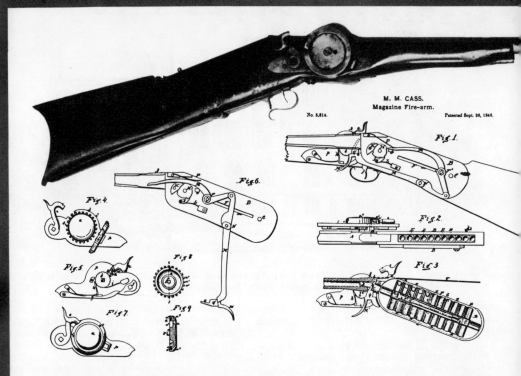

Milo M. Cass, of Utica, New York, submitted an "improved self-loading and self-capping repeating firearm," on September 26, 1848. It's a magazine rifle, 51" overall length, .38 caliber. The heavy stock contains the magazine, the cartridges are set upright, and fed forward into the firing mechanism. On the right side there is a disk that revolves automatically by operation of hammer.

sign would have made cylinders so produced inordinately expensive.

Colt, in his Letter of Patent #1304 of August, 1839, accomplished this more simply by chamfering or beveling the chambers and the end of the barrel as he described fully to the British engineers in his previously mentioned 1851 speech.

An examination of the Smithsonian Paterson-Colt pistol indicates that it, like other specimens of Paterson pistols, shows chamfering of the chambers, so that all Paterson production pistols would seem to conform to the 1839 patent although it is probable Colt was manufacturing this design even before the issue of the 1839 patent.

Colt's Paterson-made longarms were given their first friendly response from the military after Colt carried a supply of rifles and revolvers to Col. William S. Harney of the Second Dragoons, Fort Jupiter, Florida, during the winter of 1838. Military field tests conducted in 1837 had resulted in an unfavorable report, but Harney's enthusiasm, based on the Florida demonstrations, resulted in a sale to the Quartermaster General of fifty rifles. This, and a later sale of 100 Paterson carbines to the Navy by one of the creditors of the Paterson-Colt factory (the Patent Arms Mfg. Co.) which went into receivership, were the only Paterson-Colts sold to the government.

The Paterson-Colt patent model rifle in the Smithsonian is unique as it is thought to have been one of the early versions made by John Pearson in Baltimore. This is an experimental model thought to have been a replacement shortly after the Patent Office fire. One distinguishing characteristic is the resemblance to a Pennsylvania rifle with its wood forestock. The cylinder has ten chambers of approximately .33 caliber. The 31-inch barrel is rifled with seven grooves. The cylinder features a sliding cover for the protection of percussion caps. The firing pin is spring-loaded, of the rebounding type such as that pic-

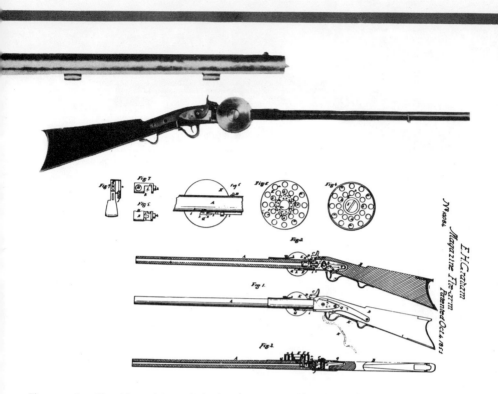

The magazine rifle with revolving cylinder here was patented by Edmund H. Graham, of Biddeford, Maine, on October 4, 1853. It's .30 caliber, has a browned barrel, 44" overall length, walnut stock, smoothbore, brass butt plate. The iron cylinder attached to the right side of barrel is 3¾" in diameter; it carries two circles of chambers, 12 all told, and is covered with solid brass cap.

tured in Colt's first patent drawings. The arm generally is more lightly constructed and more complex than the production Paterson model ring-lever rifles which largely are found to be fitted with eight-chamber cylinders. Note that there is a support over the cylinder. Early models of production Paterson ring-levers were fitted with a somewhat sturdier support or bridge, though this bridge was eliminated entirely on those produced as early as 1839.

Another distinguishing feature of these later open-top Paterson ring-lever rifles was the addition of a capping indentation or notch to the right of the recoil shield.

The Paterson carbines were six-shot rather than eight or ten-shot and of .52 caliber rather than smaller caliber rifles that ranged from .32 to .46. The ring-lever was eliminated on the carbines in favor of a simplified exposed hammer. Cocking was accomplished by thumbing back the hammer rather than pulling down on the ring-lever.

There were basic objections to the Colt revolving rifles. Most damaging of these was the complaint that the shooter, who had his face far closer to the cylinder when handling a shoulder arm than he did with a revolving pistol, might be injured by bursting percussion caps. Visibility of his target was partially obliterated by smoke or fire so close to his eyes and the fear of accidental chain-fire ignition caused some shooters to feel very ill at ease handling the gun.

One inventor, Elijah Jaquith of Brattleborough, Vermont, thought he had the answer to at least a part of the criticism directed at the Colt's shoulder arms and was awarded a patent for an improvement to revolving breech firearms, July 12, 1838.

Jaquith's solution of the problem was to mount the cylinder of his revolving rifle above rather than below the barrel. Jaquith explained his approach in the following words, ". . . the chambers are in turn brought down into contact with the

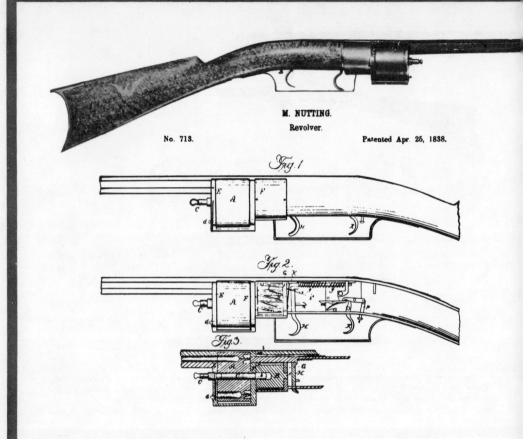

M. NUTTING.

Revolver.

No. 713.

Patented Apr. 25, 1838.

Fig. 1

Fig. 2

Fig. 3

M. Nutting patented this weapon, a revolving cylinder rifle, on April 25, 1838. It is an octagonal, rifled 29″ barrel, caliber .30, 52″ overall length. The stock is light colored wood. The small cheek piece is decorated with a brass crescent. There is a brass butt plate, a square trigger guard, and, as you will see, there are two triggers.

barrel. This arrangement, in case of any accidental ignition of the neighboring charges, renders the forward hand of the person using the gun more safe. . ." Since the shooter holds the gun with arm and hand under rather than above the barrel, Jaquith took into consideration sighting by employing a fastening or arbor through the cylinder so shaped that it filled only the lower portion allowing the shooter to sight through the cylinder above the half-round arbor. This patent was #832.

The patent model Jaquith, which is 38 inches in over-all length, with a 20-inch octagonal barrel is 6-shot, .36 caliber, with brass trim and a brass patch box. The hammer is under the frame. This model is obviously experimental as it incorporates a Pennsylvania-Kentucky type rifle stock.

Jaquith's invention never got into production, but a dozen years later, Springfield Arms Company brought out a .31 caliber 6-shot percussion-built revolver marked Jaquith's Patent, 1838. Here again a mechanism bore little resemblance to a patent claim, for the revolver has a center-hung, top-mounted hammer, conventionally located, below-the-barrel cylinder. The gun looks much like many of the Springfield Arms Company Warner's Patent, single-trigger revolvers.

For those who are interested in compli-

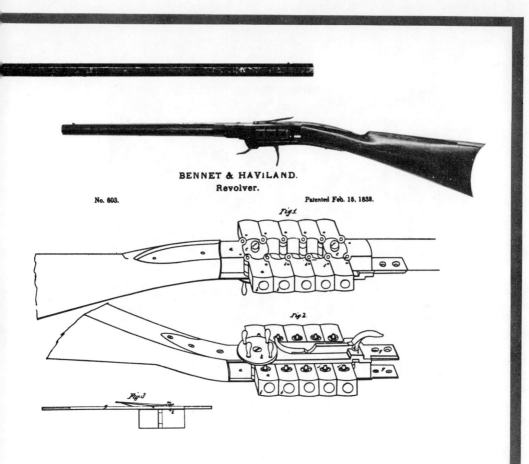

BENNET & HAVILAND.
Revolver.

No. 603.

Fig.1

Fig.2

Fig.3

Patented Feb. 15, 1838.

Patent number 603 by Haviland and Bennet, dated Feb. 15, 1838. A browned, round 8" barrel; caliber .20, overall length 20". The wood stock has a brass butt plate. The breech mechanism has three square blocks which apparently were made to slide horizontally through the frame. This one is called a miniature gun.

cated mechanisms, Epenetus A. Bennet and Frederick P. Haviland of Waterville, Maine, patented a real weirdy February 15, 1838. The patent model of Bennet and Haviland's Patent #603 is a miniaturized version of what they hoped the production model might be. Note the difference between the photo of the model and the patent drawings. The model has a round 8-inch barrel, the gun is 20 inches in over-all length, of .20 caliber with wood stock and brass butt plate. The breech mechanism of the model consists of three square brass blocks although the two inventors proposed a far larger number of blocks of steel intended to offer an endless chain of chambers with a revolving standard. Each of the blocks or chambers can move forward along the top of the gun. Each block is hinged to the next so the progression permits those blocks below the barrel to move rearward. Ultimately, each charged block chamber is brought in line with the barrel. The hammer is side-hung on the left side of the arm.

There was at least one advantage to this otherwise complicated chain-type revolving arm as a cover plate is provided for the percussion cap of the block lined up with the gun barrel so that chain-fire would be precluded or at any rate would be very unlikely. ■

PERCUSSION
–AND AFTER

It was the breakthrough. The use of fulminate of mercury—following massive experimentation— made it finally possible for the needed refinements in the development of firearms. But as with so many other inventions and developments relating to the gun, no single man was the ultimate inventor or discoverer. Here, as much as in any other field, the palm must go to all of those men— successful commercially or not—who made the tremendous effort.

THERE CAN BE no argument that the inventor must be classified among the more durable human types. Who else undergoes such a struggle, not only to invent, but to have the result of his inspiration accepted profitably by others? When one views the mountain of patent filings on firearms alone, one is filled with awe. The enterprise, the sheer tenacity of purpose, the very genius of these efforts, no matter how "far out" some may appear, is astounding. And one is brought to realize that for every patent, for every success, thousands of abortive efforts remain in wastebaskets, filing cabinets, attic trunks. Indeed, in the brisk history of firearms development, failure seems only to spur the tenacious inventor to greater effort. In consequence, the development of today's weapons was inevitable, and without question it has been, and is, a fantastic story.

High on the list of those who made irrevocable contributions to the development of "the gun" was the Reverend Alexander John Forsyth. The Reverend Forsyth's dates are 1768 to 1843. According to all evidence, the Reverend was a man of outstanding capabilities and enterprise. His interest in developing a gun lock different from what was available at the time came as the result of a hunting trip not far from his home. The young minister observed that a number of birds he was shooting at escaped his fire by diving the instant they saw the flash from the pan of his flint fowling piece. The Reverend Forsyth had heard of some experiments then going on with new primings and gun powders. He reasoned that there might possibly be a way to develop a gun that would fire fast enough to get those wily birds.

The new substances to which Forsyth turned his attention were fulminates—salts that result from metals which dissolve in acids. The Reverend Forsyth thought he could use an explosive to set off a charge. It was not so easy to build a lock that would do this, but the minister was not one to be put off by the tediousness of endless experimenting. Success finally came in 1805. He developed a pivoted magazine which deposited some fulminate in a channel leading to the bore; and a hammer which when it struck closed all possible escape for the flame, which, of course, had always been a problem.

Forsyth continued to work on improvements, and other inventors were also hard at work. The Forsyth patent, April 11, 1807, covered all forms of fulminate as well as methods of their use. Among the new inventions were patch primers, wedge primers, disc primers, straw primers, tube locks, pill locks, and so on and so forth. But the big event was the percussion cap. In a number of ways the percussion cap was the direct parent, or grandparent, of the modern metallic cartridge.

Developed by a number of people, notably Joshua Shaw, an English artist who had emigrated to America circa 1817, the copper percussion cap was an excellent primer. The metal casing was thin, and shaped rather like a top hat. A disc of tin foil covered some fulminate of mercury or potassium chlorate. In order to make it waterproof a seal of shellac was used. The cap was placed on a tube or nipple that led to the charge in the bore. The hammer struck a brisk blow and the resulting explosion drove a flame into the charge. One of the beauties of the system was that it was not at all hindered by inclement weather. Indeed, provided the charge in the barrel was kept dry, one could fire a percussion-cap gun in pelting rain. This was a tremendous advantage, especially to the military.

Moreover, it was now possible for a novice to acquire good, or at least adequate, shooting ability in a shorter time than was formerly possible, for instance with the old flintlock. The double-barreled percussion shotgun was used by sporting folk as well as the military for about three-quarters of a century. And it was used with efficiency in the gingery days of the Old West.

It was with the handgun of course that the percussion system had dramatic effect. Notable amongst those early pistol makers who worked with the new system was Henry Deringer, Jr. Henry Deringer, Jr., was a Pennsylvania gunmaker famous for his craftsmanship. For a number of years he had been making arms for the government, as well as for private sale. It is recorded that about the year 1825 he began to concentrate on percussion pistols. At first he made large pistols, but shortly concentrated on a much smaller weapon. There was a definite need for the small gun that could be hidden about one's person. Individuals in all walks of life carried the little weapon. Thieves, gamblers, congressmen, men of business, ladies of the demi-monde, all had one of the tiny pocket pistols.

Mister Deringer unfortunately had not patented his design. He had presented a firearm that had tremendous popular appeal and as a result imitators flooded the scene with their products. Presently, there were pocket pistols everywhere. It was "the thing." Yet, such was the fame of Henry Deringer's design, coupled with his name, that those imitators were forced to use his

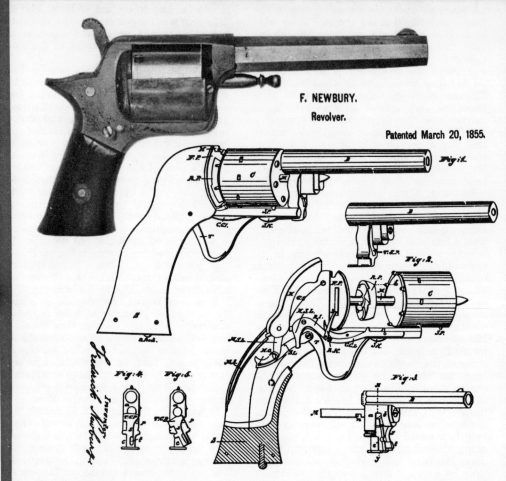

F. NEWBURY.

Revolver.

Patented March 20, 1855.

Frederick Newbury, of Albany, N. Y., patented this arm on March 20, 1855. It is numbered 12,555, and is a double-action revolver. It has a ratchet plate and ratchet lever revolving mechanism; uses two stop levers below the cylinder.

name in selling their product. Some copied his name directly, while others changed the spelling to Derringer or sometimes Beringer, or Herringer. To the public all single-shot pocket pistols were Derringers, and the common spelling that has survived is *Derringer,* with two *R's;* while *Deringer* with one *R* refers only to the pistol made by Henry Deringer, Jr.

The Derringer was a small, compact, but quite lethal weapon. The length ran from 3¾ inches to 9 inches, while calibers ranged from .33 to .51. They were, in consequence of their short barrels, not very effective,

that is to say accurate, at long range. But at close quarters, across a card table or in milady's boudoir they were deadly. It will be remembered that Abraham Lincoln was assassinated with a Derringer.

Patent #58,525 at the Smithsonian, dated October 2, 1866, is for a Derringer made by David Williamson of New York City. This was a single load breech pistol, and with its full wood stock bears a close resemblance to the Henry Deringer design. It has a brass frame 2½" barrel and is 5" in overall length. This redoubtable weapon features a .41 caliber steel sleeve with nip-

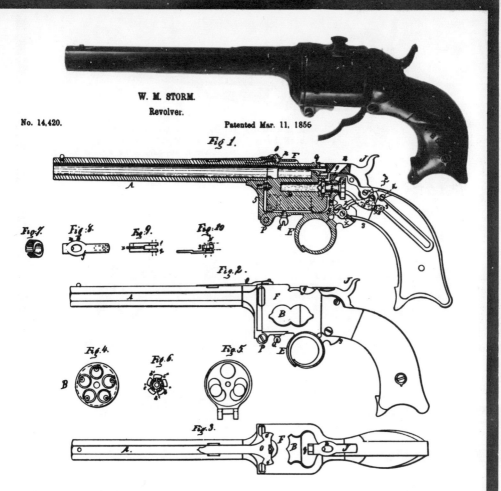

W. M. STORM.
Revolver.

No. 14,420.

Patented Mar. 11, 1856

Fig 1.

Fig 7. Fig 8. Fig 9. Fig 10.

Fig 2.

Fig 4. Fig 6. Fig 5.

Fig 3.

The weapon above is patent number 14,420 and was submitted by Wm. Mt. Storm of New York, N. Y. Dated March 11, 1856. It's an octagonal 5⅛" barrel, with overall length of 10¾"; caliber .35, and has a 5-chambered revolving cylinder.

ple fitted to the rear so that the sleeve can be loaded with cap and ball permitting the arm to handle either percussion or fixed ammunition, a distinct advantage for several years during the transition period between those two ignition systems.

But the Derringer, of course, was only one side of the story. Every imaginable type of firearm found its way to the Smithsonian files. Most gun collectors are familiar with the Cochran "monitor" pistol, a horizontal cylinder multishot (usually seven) under-hammer design, manufactured by C. B. Allen in limited numbers between

1836 and 1841. The Cochran horizontal firearms were made in both rifle and revolver format. Generally, the Cochran patent is referred to as an 1837 patent when, in actuality, the mechanism initially claimed under that patent applied to cannon and was described by its inventor as a many-chambered cannon. Issue date was October 22, 1834. We have reproduced the patent drawing here as proof that patents issued prior to the July 4, 1836 Patent Act did not necessarily carry a patent number for, as you will note, the Cochran Letters of Patent were unnumbered.

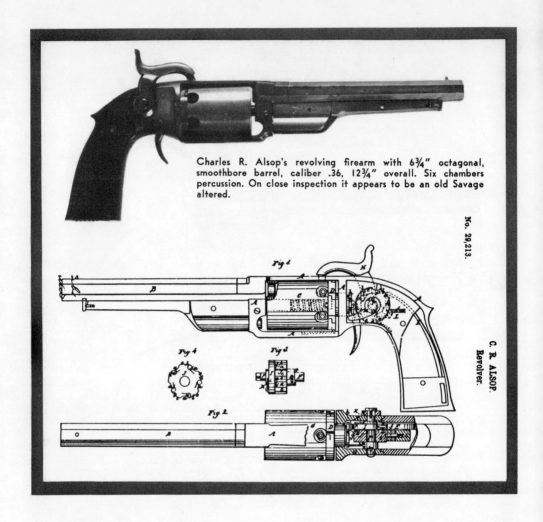

Charles R. Alsop's revolving firearm with 6¾" octagonal, smoothbore barrel, caliber .36, 12¾" overall. Six chambers percussion. On close inspection it appears to be an old Savage altered.

No. 29,213.

C. R. ALSOP.
Revolver.

The machine gun of R. J. Gatling on the other hand, was numbered 36,836; issue date was November 4, 1862. This was a six-barrel gun, the inventor having used six ordinary rifle barrels supported by an ordinary gun carriage.

Dr. Richard J. Gatling, a physician who apparently never practiced medicine, used percussion caps for ignition. The paper cartridges were held in steel containers. Gatling shortly went to copper rather than paper and also switched to rimfire. After much trial the inventor finally had his weapon accepted by the military, and it wasn't long before his name became synonymous with machine gun.

George Elgin's pistol knives or cutlasses are among the rarest collectors' items, and they are ably represented in the Smithsonian collection. Elgin patent #254 of July 5, 1837, covered a combining of a pistol and blade ". . . in such a manner that it can be used with as much ease and facility as either the pistol, knife, or cutlass could be if separate, and in an engagement, when the pistol is discharged, the knife (or cutlass) can be brought into immediate use without changing or drawing, as the two instruments are in the hand at the same time."

The United States Navy bought 150 Elgin cutlass pistols. These were .54 caliber, single-shot, with 5-inch long, smoothbore octagonal barrels, slightly over 15 inches in total length. They had side-hammer action, and iron frames. The knife trigger guard and hilt were all once piece. The Smithsonian model is similar to the 150 Navy issue which were provided for personnel under command of Lt. Charles Wilkes, who

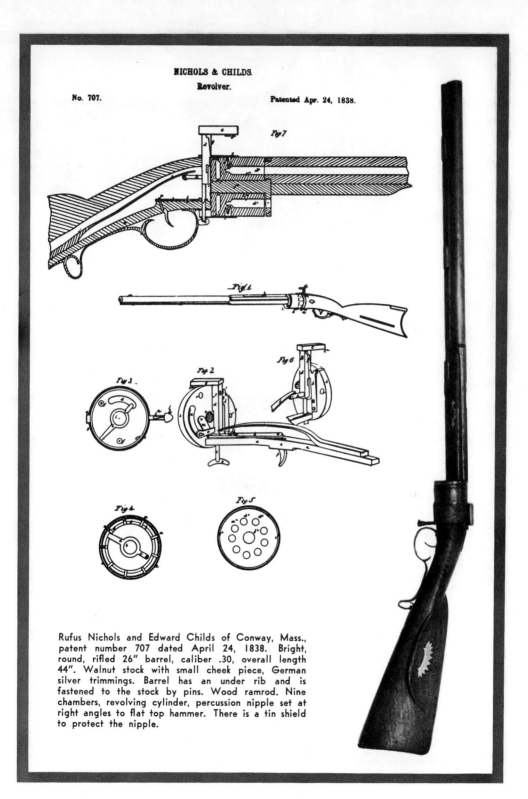

NICHOLS & CHILDS.
Revolver.

No. 707.   Patented Apr. 24, 1838.

Fig 7

Fig 1

Fig 2   *Fig 6*

Fig 3

Fig 4   *Fig 5*

Rufus Nichols and Edward Childs of Conway, Mass.,
patent number 707 dated April 24, 1838. Bright,
round, rifled 26" barrel, caliber .30, overall length
44". Walnut stock with small cheek piece, German
silver trimmings. Barrel has an under rib and is
fastened to the stock by pins. Wood ramrod. Nine
chambers, revolving cylinder, percussion nipple set at
right angles to flat top hammer. There is a tin shield
to protect the nipple.

The handgun above was patented by James Warner of Springfield, Massachusetts; date is January 7, 1851. A revolving pistol with 6" barrel, blued, round, rifled; caliber .41. It is 12½" overall, 6-chambered, single-action, percussion lock.

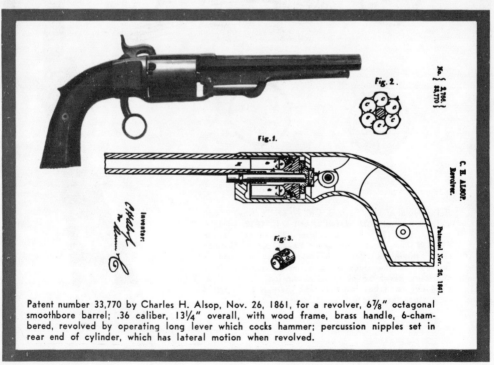

Patent number 33,770 by Charles H. Alsop, Nov. 26, 1861, for a revolver, 6⅞" octagonal smoothbore barrel; .36 caliber, 13¼" overall, with wood frame, brass handle, 6-chambered, revolved by operating long lever which cocks hammer; percussion nipples set in rear end of cylinder, which has lateral motion when revolved.

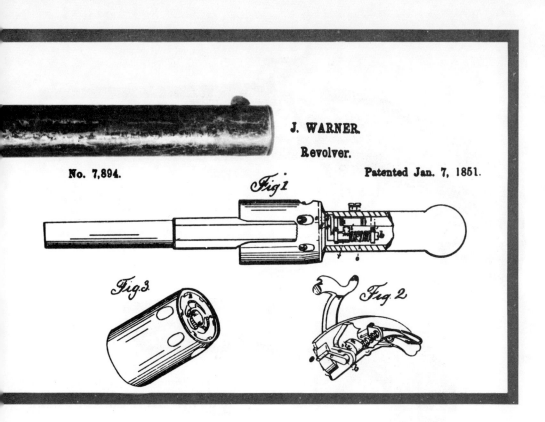

J. WARNER.

Revolver.

No. 7,894.

Patented Jan. 7, 1851.

Fig 1

Fig 3

Fig 2

headed an around-the-world naval expedition which left Virginia in August of 1838 and completed its circuit, arriving in New York June 9, 1842. During a stopover at Manila Bay in the Philippine Islands, two officers of Wilkes' crew were set upon by natives and were killed. Wilkes sent a task force ashore killing 57 natives in retaliation. This is thought to be the only military action in which the Elgin cutlass pistols were used prior to the Civil War, when some are thought to have been carried as side arms.

The Elgin pistol with the metal loop from butt to rear of the trigger guard, was of the type manufactured by C. B. Allen of Springfield. Allen apparently stressed production of the off-beat type weapon, for he was at the same time manufacturer of the J. W. Cochran ferret pistols.

A second version of the Elgin patent is marked N. P. Ames Cutler, Springfield, on the right side of the knife, Elgin's patent on the left, and on the pistol frame, C. B. Allen, Springfield, Mass. Ames later manufactured Jenks' carbines and rifles.

Although both of the Smithsonian models were pistols built by C. B. Allen, other Elgin patent arms were also made by Mor-

rill, Mossman and Blair through July of 1838, and by Mossman and Blair following Morrill's retirement through February of 1839 when the firm became bankrupt and failed.

Varying types of edged weapons combined with firearms had been made since the time of the matchlock. In the Smithsonian collection are two additional edged weapons combined with pistols. These two patents were issued four years apart, 1862 and 1866, to Robert J. Colvin of Lancaster, Pennsylvania, and to August Rauh of Westphalia, Prussia. They both concern combining revolving pistols with sword blades, with trigger mechanisms using the hilt of the sword as a guard.

The earlier of the two, the Colvin model, features a 40-inch long cavalry saber in an iron scabbard. Forward of the guard is a 6-chambered revolving cylinder pistol with a 1¾-inch barrel. The patent model is .20 caliber. The barrel is located above the blade of the sword. It's operated by a trigger inside the guard. Colvin attached the ramrod to the scabbard. A lieutenant in the Army, Colvin was doomed to disappointment for there is no record to indicate that his saber-revolver combination was ever

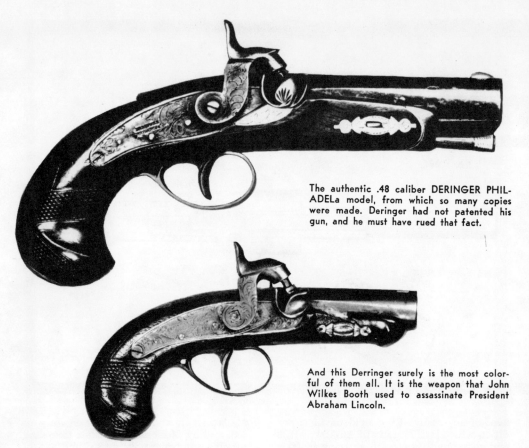

The authentic .48 caliber DERINGER PHIL-ADELa model, from which so many copies were made. Deringer had not patented his gun, and he must have rued that fact.

And this Derringer surely is the most colorful of them all. It is the weapon that John Wilkes Booth used to assassinate President Abraham Lincoln.

produced. Colvin tried again with no more success with a gun-bayonet combination two years later.

Rauh's patent varies in that the 5-inch barrel of his six-chambered .40 caliber revolver is secured to the right-hand side of the sword blade, and the hammer is side-mounted. The blade forms the base pin upon which the cylinder rotates.

Rauh's patent of February 6, 1866 was numbered 52,504. The sword blade was actually a 36-inch cavalry saber, and kept in an iron scabbard. The percussion hammer and trigger were inside the scabbard.

On June 17, 1856, Henry S. North of Middletown, Connecticut, filed Letters of Patent #15,144. This was for an improvement "in repeating firearms." North's revolver had a 6⅛" octagonal, rifled barrel. The weapon was .39 caliber, 13 inches overall length, had a brass frame, six chambers, with a wooden handle, curved top hammer, and ring trigger that operated the cylinder.

North had worked out a number of new features including a toggle connection between the cylinder and the stock that would allow the longitudinal movement of the cylinder so that it would clear the barrel when it revolved.

With Edward Savage, North designed some unique percussion revolvers. In most of the models the Savage-North percussions had brass frames, but the more distinctive feature was the figure-8-type trigger. The uppermost loop of the figure-8 trigger mechanism contains the actual trigger itself. The lower ring trigger, when pulled toward the butt, draws the cylinder away from the barrel without revolving the cylinder. Releasing the lower ring causes the cylinder to rotate and at the same time move forward into a firing position, fitting the barrel snugly and forming a nearly gas-tight, flash-proof seal. Like most of the percussions of the mid-50s and later, the .36 caliber Savage fired either loose powder and ball or a combustible paper or linen cartridge.

Henry S. North was the designer of this mechanism in 1856 and the Savage-North revolvers were made by Edward Savage at Middletown, Connecticut, until 1859. With

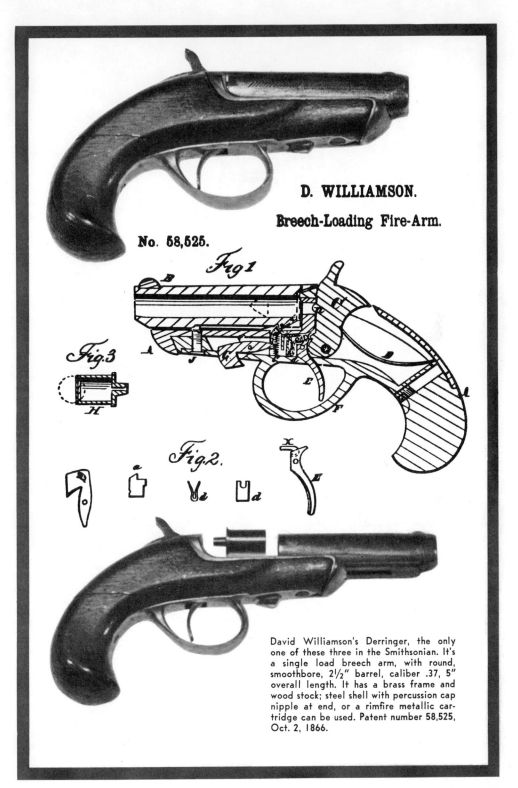

D. WILLIAMSON.

Breech-Loading Fire-Arm.

No. 58,525.

Fig 1

Fig.3

Fig.2.

David Williamson's Derringer, the only one of these three in the Smithsonian. It's a single load breech arm, with round, smoothbore, 2½" barrel, caliber .37, 5" overall length. It has a brass frame and wood stock; steel shell with percussion cap nipple at end, or a rimfire metallic cartridge can be used. Patent number 58,525, Oct. 2, 1866.

J. ELLS.
Revolver.

No. 10,812.

Patented April 25, 1851.

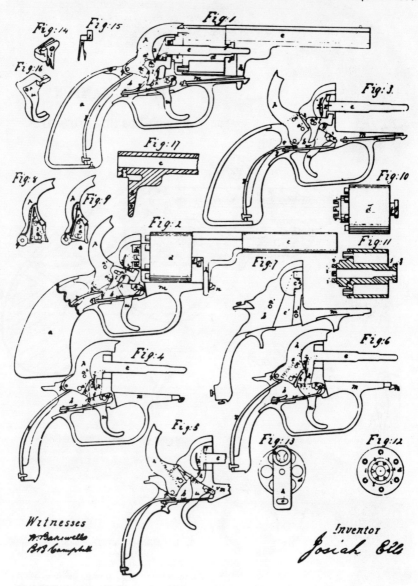

Fig. 14   Fig. 15   Fig. 1   Fig. 3   Fig. 16   Fig. 8   Fig. 9   Fig. 17   Fig. 10   Fig. 2   Fig. 11   Fig. 7   Fig. 6   Fig. 4   Fig. 5   Fig. 13   Fig. 12

Witnesses
W. Barwell
B. B. Campbell

Inventor
Josiah Ells

Josiah Ells' round, smoothbore, 4¼" barrel, caliber .30, 6-chambered automatically revolving cylinder, percussion cap nipples, brass trigger guard. The cylinder has a ¼" tubular extension surrounded by a collar that fits into a recess at breech of the barrel, which fastens the barrel to the cylinder and prevents fouling of the mechanism by smoke from the exploded cartridges.

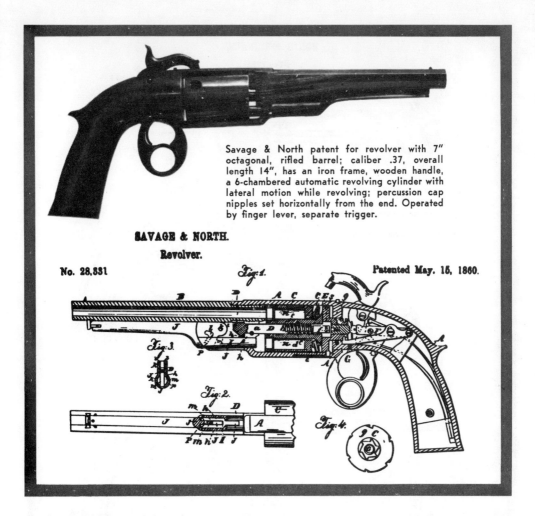

Savage & North patent for revolver with 7" octagonal, rifled barrel; caliber .37, overall length 14", has an iron frame, wooden handle, a 6-chambered automatic revolving cylinder with lateral motion while revolving; percussion cap nipples set horizontally from the end. Operated by finger lever, separate trigger.

SAVAGE & NORTH.

Revolver.

No. 28,331

Fig. 1.

Patented May. 15, 1860.

Fig. 3.

Fig. 2.

Fig. 4.

jointly improved patents the two men formed the Savage Repeating Firearms Corporation in 1860. The 1860 models included several improvements, one of which was a huge trigger guard covering the figure-8 and extending down almost to the bottom of the grip frame. The distinctive spur on the back of the grip was eliminated. The grip frame itself was made wider and when the gun also included some other improvements, the Navy purchased nearly 11,300.

There are five North, North & Savage, North & Skinner patents at the Smithsonian, but such is the richness of the collection that we are, unfortunately, not able to include every item in these pages.

One of the least frequently seen percussion revolvers is a bar hammer, 5-shot Ells, patented by Josiah Ells of Pittsburgh, Pennsylvania. Ells manufactured this and

four similar revolvers as well as a ring-trigger single shot, for less than three years. Very few specimens of Ells' arms still exist. There is a very nice Ells in the Harolds Club collection at Reno, Nevada. It's a rare item; full-framed, bar-hammer percussion with a piece at the frame shoulder which protected the shooter from flashback.

On April 24, 1838, Rufus Nichols and Edward Childs of Conway, Massachusetts, patented a manually revolved cylinder type percussion revolver and revolving rifle. A lever located on the side of the frame was used to align the cylinder with the barrel and to force it forward to provide a "gas tight seal." The Nichols & Childs seal was not really gas tight, however.

James Warner of Springfield, Massachusetts, patented a mechanism, or system whereby the chambers of a revolving chambered pistol would be revolved by the

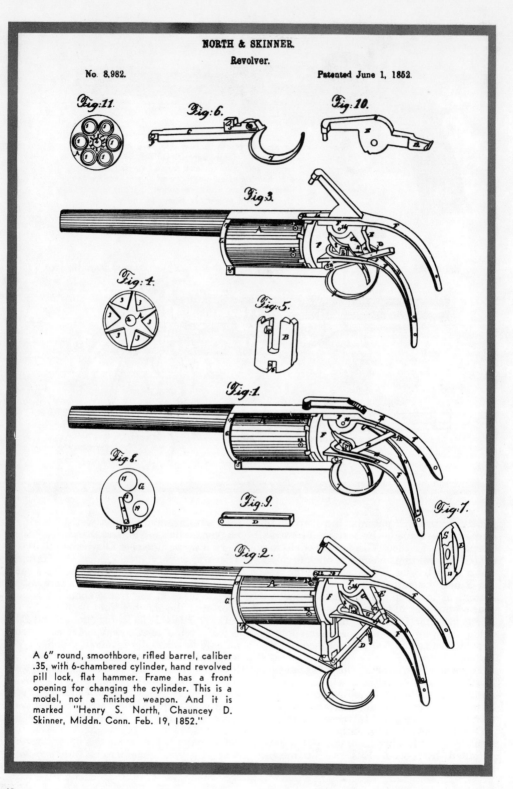

NORTH & SKINNER.
Revolver.

No. 8,982.

Patented June 1, 1852.

Fig:11.

Fig:6.

Fig:10.

Fig:3.

Fig:4.

Fig:5.

Fig:1.

Fig:8.

Fig:9.

Fig:7.

Fig:2.

A 6″ round, smoothbore, rifled barrel, caliber .35, with 6-chambered cylinder, hand revolved pill lock, flat hammer. Frame has a front opening for changing the cylinder. This is a model, not a finished weapon. And it is marked "Henry S. North, Chauncey D. Skinner, Middn. Conn. Feb. 19, 1852."

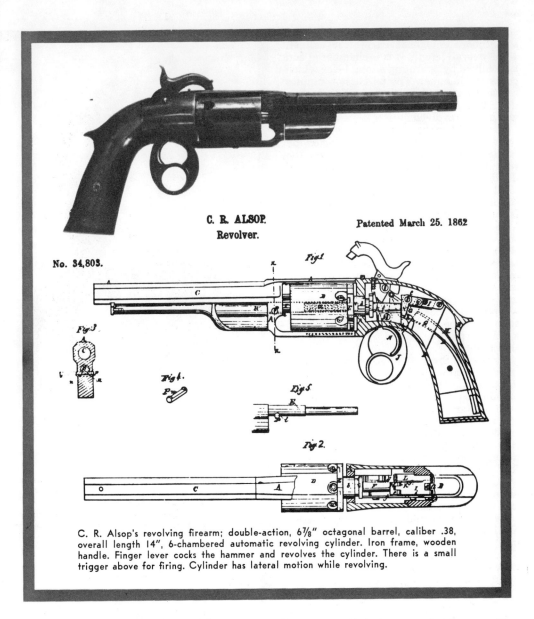

C. R. ALSOP.
Revolver.

No. 34,803.

Patented March 25. 1862

Fig 1

Fig 3

Fig 4.

Fig 5

Fig 2.

C. R. Alsop's revolving firearm; double-action, 6⅞" octagonal barrel, caliber .38, overall length 14", 6-chambered automatic revolving cylinder. Iron frame, wooden handle. Finger lever cocks the hammer and revolves the cylinder. There is a small trigger above for firing. Cylinder has lateral motion while revolving.

action of a lever of which the fulcrum or axis of vibration was in line with the axis of rotation of the chamber; thus revolving the chambers with greater certainty. Warner's patent was number 7,894 dated January 7, 1851. His revolving pistol had a 6-inch barrel, was round, blued, rifled; caliber .41, 6-chambered single-action percussion lock, 12½ inches overall length. The model is marked "Springfield Arms Co."

Patent number 29,213 of July 17, 1860, is listed for Charles R. Alsop of Middletown, Connecticut. It is for a revolving arm with a 6¾" octagonal, smoothbore barrel, .36 caliber, 12¾" overall length. The arm has a wooden hand grip, brass frame, and is 6-chamber percussion. There's a cam at the rear of the cylinder which combines with the hammer by means of a ratchet and pawl. This allows part of a revolution by cocking the hammer, permitting the cylinder to move back from the barrel to free the turn. At the end of the turn, or revolution, the cylinder moves forward.

Patent number 33,770 for Charles H. Alsop is for a revolving firearm with a 6⅞" smoothbore octagonal barrel, .36 caliber, 13¼" overall length. It is 6-chambered and is revolved by operating a long lever which cocks the hammer. The percussion nipples are set horizontally in the rear of the cylinder. The cylinder has a lateral motion when it is revolved.

Two additional percussion developments were to round out the work started by Alexander Forsyth. One of these was the tape primer, invented by a Washington dentist, Dr. Edward Maynard. The Maynard primer operated not unlike the cap pistol roll with which every American boy is familiar. A number of pellets of fulminate of mercury were evenly spaced along strips of paper then covered by another strip of paper and the entire unit sealed and shellacked. Maynard also developed a magazine to hold these caps plus a mechanism to feed the tape. Every time the hammer of a Maynard tape magazine equipped weapon was cocked a fresh section of the strip would be automatically reeled out and a pellet would be placed over the percussion nipple.

In 1845 at Springfield Armory 300 muskets were altered to accept the Maynard multicapping primer. By 1848 thousands of additional conversions were made by both military and private rifle owners.

With the government acceptance of percussion as replacement for flintlock, the rifle was finally also given definite recognition as being superior to the smoothbore. Still the military lagged behind the civilians. The then-new percussion muskets were still largely muzzleloaders with ball and powder loads.

As early as the mid-17th century Swedes had been using paper cartridges containing ball and powder in one packaged unit. The paper-wrapped bullet and powder which was in a single cylinder was a very useful item for loading by the muzzle, since the cardboard or paper tube which held the charge could easily be opened so that the powder could be poured in, the bullet dropped in and then the wrapper used to wad the load and seat it firmly in place.

This bullet was shortly followed by a bullet and powder unit that was also paper-encased but designed so that it could be loaded without the necessity of unwrapping. The paper, being nitrated, was consumed in the firing.

Yet another advance was to come. This was by Christian Sharps, whose rifle became the scourge of the bison of the American Plains. Sharps' cartridges, which consisted of loose powder and bullet, were

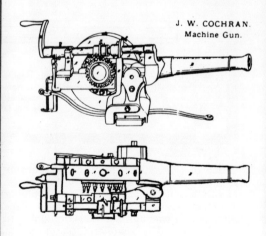

J. W. COCHRAN.
Machine Gun.

The J. W. Cochran patent drawing for a machine gun, unnumbered. It was described by its inventor as a many-chambered cannon.

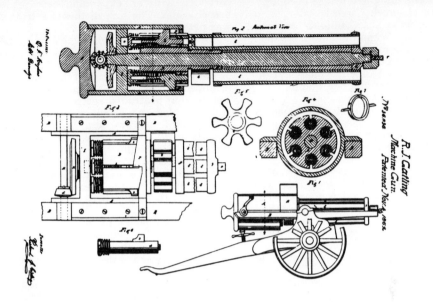

Richard J. Gatling, at left, a doctor who, it appears, never practiced medicine. But this was the gain for firearms. His name has become synonymous with "machine gun"; and his patent drawing #36,836 is reproduced here, dated November 4, 1862, with photograph below. This was a 6-barrel gun, with breech closed by a wooden disc. Overall length was 36 inches; 20½" gun carriage, width 23".

wrapped in linen which was treated. They were originally designed for use in Sharps' falling breech-block breechloader, and were not nearly as susceptible to breaking open in handling. When the Sharps weapon was held with the muzzle down, the breech was opened. When the cartridge was placed inside, the sharp edge of the block cut off one end of the linen wrapper, and exposed the charge of powder. Then, either a percussion cap, or later, as it developed, a Maynard tape primer, specially adapted for the Sharps, ignited charge. The treated linen was consumed during ignition.

It is interesting to note that two factors marked a mid-century flurry in percussion revolver production. The first of these was the expiration of Colt's basic percussion revolver patents in 1856. The other influence was the tremendous increase in demand for firearms caused by the brawling westward expansion from the time of the discovery of gold in 1848 on through to the military requirements of the Civil War. While many of the dozens of manufacturers who turned to sixshooters in 1856 did so with original, even weird, designs, others such as the Manhattan Arms Company, Metropolitan, Walch and Cooper closely copied Colt's products.

Models of nearly all of the manufacturers mentioned were also in use by the Confederate forces. During the combat days of the Civil War one of the best made of the Confederate arms was the Leech and Rigdon. This sixshooter percussion was a direct imitation of the Colt six-shot, caliber .36, the Colt Navy Model 1861. The output of these arms was tremendous and the Leech and Rigdon quality was high—considered to be the equivalent of that of Colt.

But really successful breechloaders arrived on the scene only when an efficient metal cartridge was developed. To be sure, the metallic cartridge was no big news in the 1800s. It had even been experimented with a century earlier, although it had not yet found its place. The notion of a metal cartridge that would be flexible, with the case expanding when the gun was fired so that leakage would be sealed off, was not seriously considered until the middle of the 19th century.

The redoubtable Sam Colt had worked along these lines, notably on a metal foil-covered cartridge. His idea had been to prevent spoilage of the paper-wrapped powder charge which was due to absorption of water. Strangely, safety in handling, rapidity of loading, and waterproofing were considered more important than the really more important problem of sealing the breech.

Then, Dr. Maynard designed a metallic cartridge with an expanding case for a breechloader. The first of these cartridges was patented in 1856.

Pin or tit-fire cartridges, which were encased in metal with a small rod-like projection extending vertically just in front of the base were the earliest that included priming as well as soft expanding walls. The tit that protruded served as an anvil, and exploded the priming charge in the shell when it was struck.

Early in the 19th century, Captain Minie, a French Army officer, created a conical-shaped bullet, first with a solid base, and later with a hollow conical base which expanded on firing and offered gas-sealing properties. His bullet became exceedingly popular.

In 1847, another Frenchman, named Flobert, developed a rimfire cartridge called a B-B cap. B-B stood for bullet breech. The rimfire design of the Flobert cartridges was just about the same as today's rimfire cartridges. A copper disc was punched out and drawn on dies into a closed tube. The rim was worked into shape at one end. The hollow rim which was at the base of the cap held the priming charge, which was usually fulminate of mercury. When the hammer struck, the priming charge was set off and the powder charge fired.

In the United States Smith & Wesson developed Flobert's B-B cap into what eventually became the .22 short rimfire cartridge.

Although the military had accepted breechloaders in small quantities, the bulk of the issue of military weapons were muzzle loaders. During the Civil War muskets left on the battlefields were frequently found to be loaded, some with as many as a half dozen or more loads, one superimposed on top of the other. The explanation was an obvious one. While man may undergo a certain excitement in taking a pot shot at a deer, his excitement doesn't begin to compare with that which he experiences when his intended target is armed and fires back at him. In the din of battle misfires frequently went unnoticed and firearms were rendered useless or in some instances, casualties occurred during the excitement by charging the weapons with more than one load. It became apparent that for combat a more foolproof weapon was necessary, particularly with paper cartridges which could, without care, be loaded ball-end down and thus not catch fire even though the priming charge exploded properly.

As always with firearms, the need was answered. ■

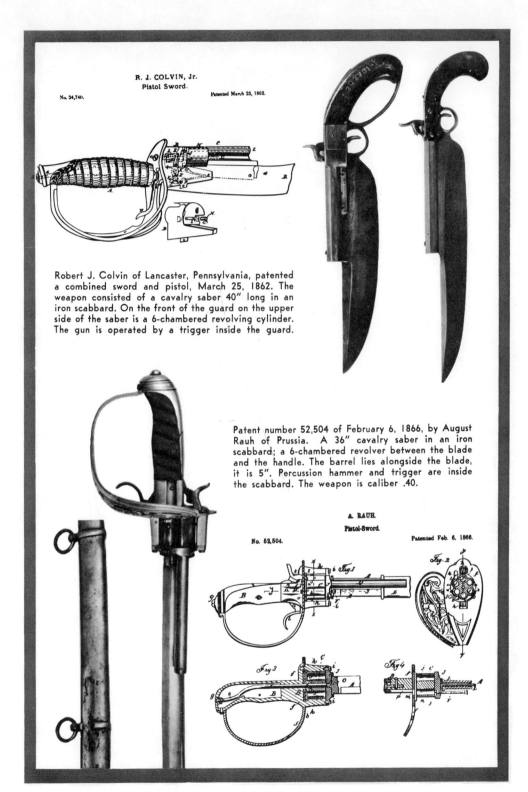

R. J. COLVIN, Jr.
Pistol Sword.

No. 34,740.

Patented March 25, 1862.

Robert J. Colvin of Lancaster, Pennsylvania, patented a combined sword and pistol, March 25, 1862. The weapon consisted of a cavalry saber 40" long in an iron scabbard. On the front of the guard on the upper side of the saber is a 6-chambered revolving cylinder. The gun is operated by a trigger inside the guard.

Patent number 52,504 of February 6, 1866, by August Rauh of Prussia. A 36" cavalry saber in an iron scabbard; a 6-chambered revolver between the blade and the handle. The barrel lies alongside the blade, it is 5". Percussion hammer and trigger are inside the scabbard. The weapon is caliber .40.

A. RAUH.
Pistol-Sword.

No. 52,504.

Patented Feb. 6, 1866.

THE BREECH

Obviously, to load at the breech would be quicker, easier, safer than loading in the old way—from the muzzle. But there were hazards. To begin with, another opening in the barrel would be necessary, but then, such an opening would have to close in such a manner that flame and gases could not escape. Without a tight seal at the breech there would be danger to the shooter, and moreover, the bullet would lack power. But the search was on.

THE BREECHLOADER, already long accepted by civilian hunters, was not subject to multiple loading disasters due to nerves, forgetfulness or sheer panic; although the self-consuming cartridge could be loaded ball end hindmost just as with the muzzle-loader. The lack of a satisfactory bullet, in addition to the inherent breech leaks, however, was the deterrent to a faster development of the breechloader.

Quite obviously it was faster to load from the breech than from the muzzle; it was also easier. One could lie down to load from the breech; there was not all that business of putting powder, ball, and wadding down the end of the muzzle from the front end, and ramming it.

Of course, to load from the breech required another opening in the barrel, and such an opening would have to close tightly, so that gases and flame could not escape. The bullet would not only derive less power from such a faulty opening, but would also be dangerous for the shooter. Developing something that would open and shut quickly and easily and at the same time be tight, however, was no easy matter.

Although the United States Military was not to adopt a breechloading shoulder arm until the early 1800s, much experimentation had gone on in that line. The Dutch had perfected a breechloading cartridge gun in 1725. Around the end of the 17th century an Englishman named John Willmore had developed a screw-plug-type breech mechanism. Then in 1720 John Warsop, another Englishman, built a flintlock breechloading rifle.

The Warsop rifle breech mechanism had a screw-threaded plug at right angles to the bore. The plug was larger than the bore and was attached to the forward end of the trigger guard. The plug, with the attached trigger guard, screwed into the barrel from below. The screw-plug on the Warsop rifle had a single thread and it took 4¼ revolutions of the trigger guard to screw the plug completely home. Also, since the screw-plug did not go completely through the barrel, the Warsop screw-plug breechloader required that the plug be taken completely out of the barrel in order to load.

In 1776 Patrick Ferguson, a Scotsman, refined the Warsop mechanism and designed the Ferguson rifle. Ferguson was a soldier, an officer in the British army at the age of 14. He was born in 1744, the second son of James Pitfour, a laird of Aberdeenshire. At the tender age of 14 he was serving in Germany as a cornet in the Scot's Greys. Ill health forced him home in 1762,

but two years later he was back in service, against the Caribs in the West Indies. Once again he was forced by illness to return to Scotland. At the age of 30 he began really to work with firearms.

The Ferguson rifle had a screw-plug with a double thread, a great improvement over the earlier Warsop because it permitted the plug to be dropped with far less rotary movement. Ferguson also had his plug extend completely through the top of the barrel, so that when the plug was unscrewed the weapon could be loaded from the top without completely removing the screw-type breech plug. The arm was rifled with 12 deep grooves and its bore was 11/16 of an inch. The overall length of the Ferguson rifle was 52 inches, and the round barrel, flattened 6 inches from the breech, was 36⅛ inches long.

It was claimed that because of the ease of the breechloading mechanism the British infantryman could fire six shots a minute from a standing position, or four shots a minute while advancing. This was true for a rifleman who was practiced at handling a Ferguson.

A limited number of Ferguson breechloading flintlocks were adopted by the British, but Ferguson was killed in action in the Battle of Kings Mountain, October 7, 1780, by an American rifle ball fired from a muzzle-loader. His rifle was far in advance of its time, and without his drive to promote the weapon, the British military discarded it.

The first American breechloading rifle to be mass produced was the Hall. It was patented by John H. Hall, of Yarmouth, Maine, on May 21, 1811. The breech mechanism of the Hall lock was extremely simple. The breech merely tipped up to allow the chamber to be loaded with powder and ball. However, where the movable breech lined up with the barrel, there was a space of about .018 of an inch and because of this space, considerable gas leakage occurred, with the result that the Hall breechloader did not have as great a muzzle velocity as the muzzle-loaders. The overall length of the first Halls, which were made in quantity from 1819 and, with only minor variations, continued to be made through 1840, was 52⅝ inches with a 32⅝-inch barrel. Despite their lesser muzzle velocity, the Hall breechloader could be loaded and fired with greater rapidity than the muzzle-loaders, and as a consequence they were issued to use against the Indians.

Hall was without doubt an authentic genius. Not much is known about the actual origin of Hall's rifle. He asserted that he

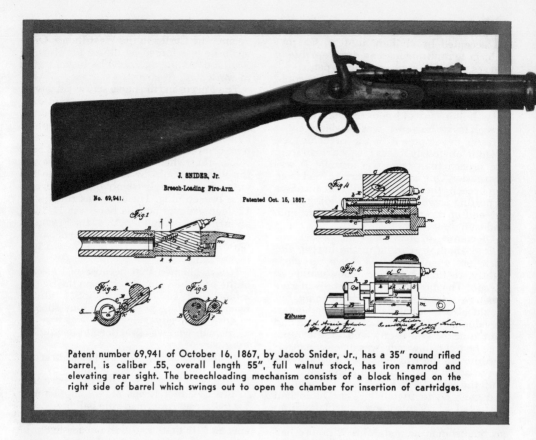

J. SNIDER, Jr.
Breech-Loading Fire-Arm.

No. 69,941.

Patented Oct. 15, 1867.

Patent number 69,941 of October 16, 1867, by Jacob Snider, Jr., has a 35" round rifled barrel, is caliber .55, overall length 55", full walnut stock, has iron ramrod and elevating rear sight. The breechloading mechanism consists of a block hinged on the right side of barrel which swings out to open the chamber for insertion of cartridges.

knew very little about rifles at the time; and so it appears that he approached his problem with a quite open mind. The Hall rifle was not only adopted by the Military but production began at once at the Harpers Ferry Armory; and the inventor himself was engaged to supervise the work.

John Hancock Hall had not only invented the actual rifle, but he also developed machinery to manufacture it on an assembly line basis which had interchangeable parts. Hall developed the first interchangeable arms in the United States, and perhaps even in the world.

Although the United States was the first country to issue an arm such as the Hall breechloader in quantity, other nations were by no means idle in that same field. All over Europe there were experiments and tests with breechloading firearms.

Among the most enterprising of the inventors and experimenters was one Samuel Johannes Pauly, a Swiss gentleman with all the fine attention to detail that is the trademark of his country. Mr. Pauly produced some interesting breechloading designs. In Paris, in the year 1812 Pauly finally came into his own as a firearms man and created and patented his first design on the 29th of September. The gun that Pauly designed had, amongst other features, an internal firing pin with a cocking lever on the outside, a break-open breech which closed with a lever on long guns, and for pistols a tip-down barrel; and, moreover, a center-fire cartridge with a paper torso and brass head.

Of course, there were imperfections, which is to be expected with any new invention. But as a consequence Pauly never reached financial success with his gun. All the same, his represented a major step forward in firearms design, and it can be successfully asserted that Pauly was one of the milestones in gun development.

During the American Civil War many breechloading systems were produced. Numerous different actions were patented and put on the market. Some were good, some were ridiculous. But the sum total of the effort was growth and development.

In 1855 A. D. Perry patented one of the many breechloading percussion rifles made after the turn of the half century. The pe-

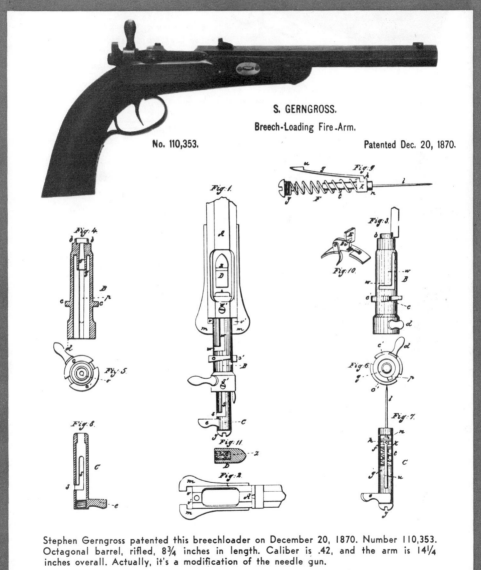

S. GERNGROSS.

Breech-Loading Fire-Arm.

No. 110,353.

Patented Dec. 20, 1870.

Stephen Gerngross patented this breechloader on December 20, 1870. Number 110,353. Octagonal barrel, rifled, 8¾ inches in length. Caliber is .42, and the arm is 14¼ inches overall. Actually, it's a modification of the needle gun.

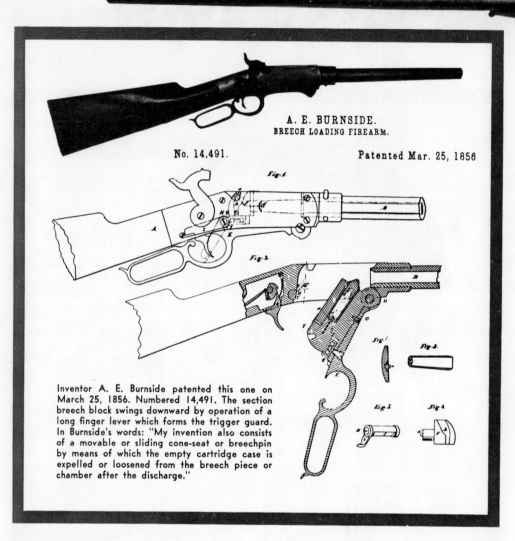

A. E. BURNSIDE.
BREECH LOADING FIREARM.

No. 14,491.

Patented Mar. 25, 1856

Fig.1.

Fig.2.

Inventor A. E. Burnside patented this one on March 25, 1856. Numbered 14,491. The section breech block swings downward by operation of a long finger lever which forms the trigger guard. In Burnside's words: "My invention also consists of a movable or sliding cone-seat or breechpin by means of which the empty cartridge case is expelled or loosened from the breech piece or chamber after the discharge."

culiarity of the Perry rifle, which was manufactured by the Perry Patent Firearms Co., of Newark, N.J., was its vibrator charge holder which contained 50 percussion caps. The lever action operated a breech working on an arbor in a socket which moved in a half circle, so that the cartridge was loaded bullet uppermost through the top of the rotating breech. Each action of the trigger guard automatically loaded a fresh percussion cap from a spring-loaded tube in the stock so the action was fast. At least 200 of these were

sold to the War Department in caliber .52. Perry used the same action in .36 and .45 caliber sporting rifles.

While the majority of service issue arms during the Civil War were muzzle-loaders many commercial breechloaders were also used. In 1848 Christian Sharps developed his famous Sharps rifle, one of the outstanding arms of the mid-nineteenth century. The Sharps action consisted of throwing forward the trigger guard, which dropped a sliding block at the rear of the barrel and uncovered the breech for load-

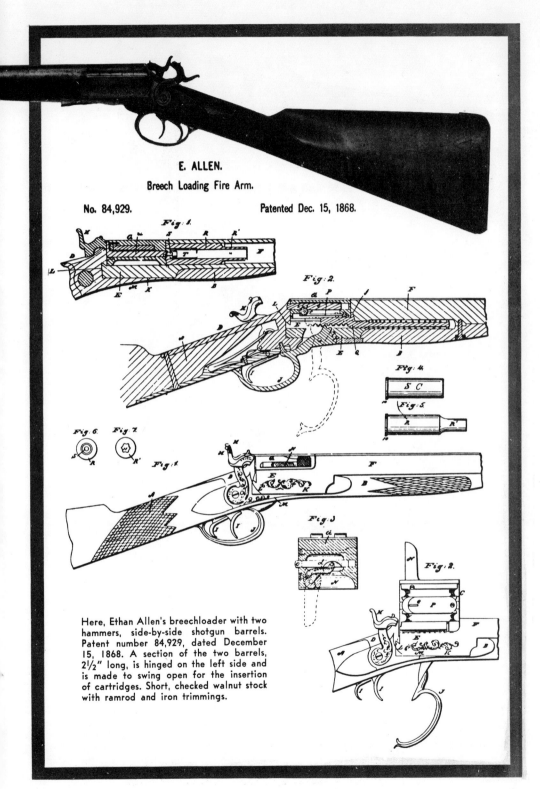

E. ALLEN.
Breech Loading Fire Arm.

No. 84,929.   Patented Dec. 15, 1868.

Here, Ethan Allen's breechloader with two hammers, side-by-side shotgun barrels. Patent number 84,929, dated December 15, 1868. A section of the two barrels, 2½" long, is hinged on the left side and is made to swing open for the insertion of cartridges. Short, checked walnut stock with ramrod and iron trimmings.

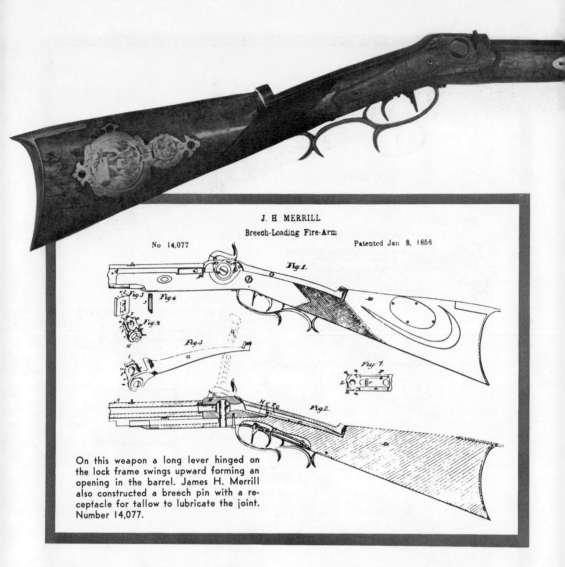

J. H MERRILL.

Breech-Loading Fire-Arm

No 14,077

Patented Jan 8, 1856

Fig 1.

Fig 3 Fig 4

Fig 4

Fig 5

Fig 7

Fig 2

On this weapon a long lever hinged on the lock frame swings upward forming an opening in the barrel. James H. Merrill also constructed a breech pin with a receptacle for tallow to lubricate the joint. Number 14,077.

ing. Paper, and later Sharps' linen cartridges were then inserted and after the trigger guard was drawn back, the rising block sheared off the rear end of the cartridge, exposing the powder charge. When the trigger guard was fully returned to position, the sliding block effectively covered the breech.

On the earlier Sharps a Maynard tape primer was used. This was improved later by the special Sharps priming disc magazine, which was further refined by Richard S. Lawrence in 1851 and is usually referred to as the Lawrence primer.

The Sharps played a big role in the West as a buffalo gun. At the same time, it was admirably suited to target shooting. At the end of the Civil War many Sharps weapons

were converted to accept the new self-contained metallic cartridges. In late 1877 an improvement by Borchardt brought a new hammerless line with an enclosed firing pin in the breech. In 1881 the Sharps Rifle Company ceased to manufacture.

In 1856 Dr. Edward Maynard had brought out an improved metal cartridge with a pointed projectile. Earlier that same year Ambrose Everett Burnside had also developed a metal-cased cartridge. Burnside also achieved fame elsewhere, as McClellan's successor in command of the Federal Army of the Potomac. And a sort of anagram of his name has come down in history. The term "sideburns" is a popular corruption of "burnsides", a style of sidewhiskers worn by, and named for, the

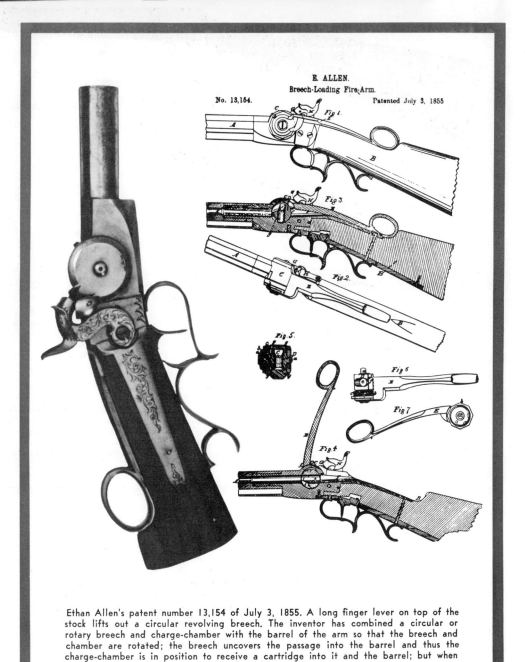

E. ALLEN.
Breech-Loading Fire-Arm.

No. 13,154.

Patented July 3, 1855

Fig 1.
Fig 3.
Fig 2.
Fig 5.
Fig 6
Fig 7
Fig 4.

Ethan Allen's patent number 13,154 of July 3, 1855. A long finger lever on top of the stock lifts out a circular revolving breech. The inventor has combined a circular or rotary breech and charge-chamber with the barrel of the arm so that the breech and chamber are rotated; the breech uncovers the passage into the barrel and thus the charge-chamber is in position to receive a cartridge into it and the barrel; but when rotated in the opposite direction, the breech covers the passage.

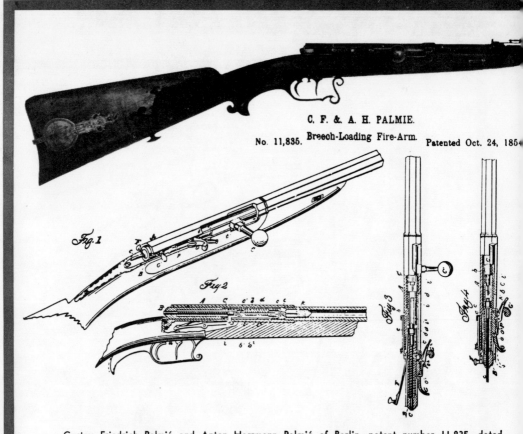

C. F. & A. H. PALMIE.
Breech-Loading Fire-Arm.
No. 11,835.   Patented Oct. 24, 1854.

Fig. 1

Fig 2

Fig 3

Fig 4

Gustav Friedrich Palmié and Anton Harrmann Palmié of Berlin, patent number 11,835, dated October 24, 1854. A needle gun. "Our invention consists in certain improvements in the touch-needle gun: first, in the formation of a valve and valve-seat upon the spring guide bar and guide for the needle to prevent the possibility of backfire; secondly, in a safety-lock to prevent the possibility of firing by accidental discharge." In other words, a cushioned valve-seat on the end of the needle-bar to close the opening through which the needle passes into the charge; and a safety locking-bolt to hold the mainspring.

General. See Burnside's patent on page 50.

Now, with the coming of the metallic cartridge the problems of the breechloader were overcome; for, upon firing, the lightweight copper or brass tube expanded and prevented blowback. Regardless of carelessness or even stupidity, the metallic cartridges, with their rims or mule ears, could not be loaded backward, even if you tried.

During the Civil War, Union Colonel Hiram Berdan, whose regiment was attached to the Army of the Potomac, had armed his men largely with Sharps Model 1859 rifles. The outstanding marksmanship of Berdan's regiment, according to

some historians, resulted in the origin of the word "sharpshooter." At the same time, the authenticity of this notion is open to argument since there is an old English print circa 1812 which, in its caption refers to a British contingent of the time as "Sharp-shooters." That is of small moment, however. The point is that Berdan, like Burnside, was a military man who contributed to the development of firearms.

When the Civil War was ended Berdan resigned from the Army in order to experiment with his own designs, which included the first center-fire, bottleneck-type cartridge, a single hinged breechlock, an improved alteration of the Model 1861 United

H. W. ADAMS.
Breech-Loading Fire-Arm.

No. 11,685.

Patented Sept. 19, 1854.

Henry W. Adams of New York, patent of September 19, 1854, number 11,685. Round, rifled 29" barrel, overall length 49", caliber .54. A long lever on the right hand side of the full wood stock moves a round block extending horizontally through the rear of the barrel and opens the way by which the cartridge can be inserted. The inventor refers to this as a "breech-roller," and claims that the roller is a movable breech, serving to open and close a fixed chamber in which the charge is contained.

States Springfield rifle to a caliber .58.

To Colonel Berdan must go the credit for the idea of die-stamping brass cartridge cases, with the anvil being made an integral part of the shell, thus reducing cost of cartridge making and also rendering safe the use of powerful charges of powder, not feasible in rimfire cartridges. Although the Berdan primer was later to be discarded in favor of a separate anvil, during the latter half of the 19th century, center-fire primers were largely of the Berdan type, and remained so in Europe for a number of years.

Like other developments, metal cartridges in the early stages were of many and varied designs. In Prussia, Dreyse developed the needle gun, an idea previously experimented with by Pauly in 1812. Dreyse's successful needle gun developed in 1838 was breechloading with a bolt action. It was fired by a long steel needle which pierced the base of the cartridge, passed through the powder charge to the fulminate pellet, which was sandwiched between wads and between the projectile and the powder.

There were three drawbacks to the Dreyse pin fire, though the arm was officially adopted by the Prussian Army. The slender, needlelike piercing striker was liable to break. A certain amount of blow-

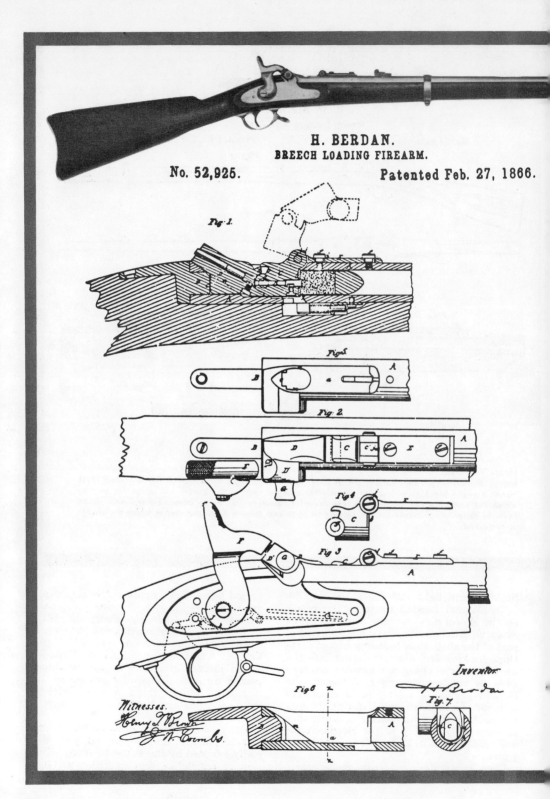

H. BERDAN.
BREECH LOADING FIREARM.

No. 52,925.

Patented Feb. 27, 1866.

Tig 1.

Fig 5

Fig 2.

Tig 4

Fig 3

Fig 6

Fig 7.

Witnesses.

Henry T. Brown
J. W. Coombs.

Inventor
H. Berdan

Colonel Hiram Berdan, of Berdan's "Sharpshooters" fame, was a man of not only military attainment, but an inventor of consequence.

Berdan's breechloading firearm was patent number 52,925, dated Feb. 27, 1866. It is a 40" round, rifled barrel, overall length of 56 inches, and caliber .58. It has a full walnut stock, and open front sight, double leaf rear sight. The breech mechanism has a double pivoted block hinged at the forward end, fitting down into the breech of the barrel. The above is an old U.S. Army musket (1861 Special Model) altered to illustrate Berdan's invention.

back also occurred through the rear of the pierced cartridge case, and finally, the powder fulminate and the burning gases combined to cause swift corrosion of the needle.

The needle gun patent in the Smithsonian is by Gustav F. and A. H. Palmié. It is dated October 24, 1854. Their invention consisted in the formation of a valve or valve-seat upon the spring guide bar, and guide for the needle to prevent the possibility of backfire. There is also a safety lock to prevent the chance of firing by accidental discharge.

Although the principal importance placed on the Dreyse arm at the time of its development was its method of percussion, collectors today are more interested in the arm because it was the first successful bolt action rifle.

In France a variation of the Dreyse needle gun was also introduced before the second half of the 19th century. This was the Chassepot, which varied from the Prussian arm by having the fulminate charge at the rear of the cartridge contained in a copper cap imbedded in the cartridge base. A washer interposed between the front face of the breech bolt and a flange or shoulder on the needle guide hermetically sealed the breech and prevented blowback. Models of both the Dreyse and Chassepot were used by Confederate forces during the Civil War but were not overly popular, largely because of the tendency of the needles to bend or break.

In 1847 Houiller of France developed a pin-fire cartridge and Le Faucheux applied this cartridge to his hinged-barrel breechloader which later developed into the present-day hinged drop-down barreled shotguns.

The pin-fire cartridge is a metal-cased cartridge with a projectile at the forward end, a powder charge in the rear and protruding from the top of the cartridge at the rear is a short anvil. The breech of the Le Faucheux is equipped with a slot through which the anvil protrudes. An overhead striking hammer drives the anvil into the fulminate cap, which is bedded down in the powder compartment.

Many Le Faucheux rifles and pistols were used by the Confederate forces during the Civil War, but primarily because of an arms shortage, for like the Chassepot and Dreyse, the pin-fire also has several weak points. The anvil protruding above the breech is subject to being accidentally struck, with a resultant untimely discharge of the bullet. The overhead hammer which swings through a decided arc to strike down on

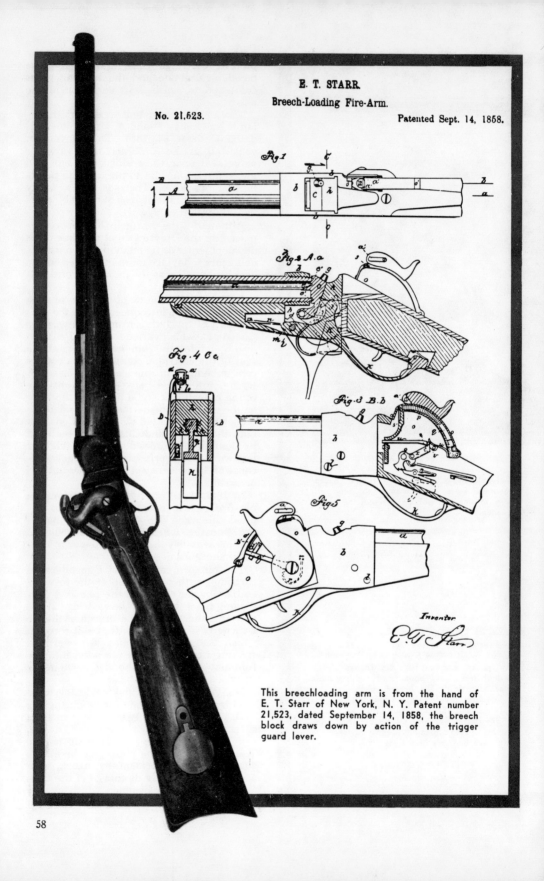

E. T. STARR.

Breech-Loading Fire-Arm.

No. 21,523.   Patented Sept. 14, 1858.

Fig 1

Fig 2 A.a

Fig. 4 C.c

Fig. 3 B.b

Fig 5

Inventor

E. T. Starr

This breechloading arm is from the hand of
E. T. Starr of New York, N. Y. Patent number
21,523, dated September 14, 1858, the breech
block draws down by action of the trigger
guard lever.

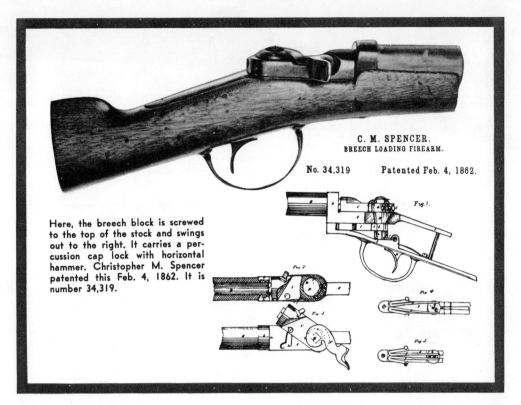

C. M. SPENCER.
BREECH LOADING FIREARM.

No. 34,319   Patented Feb. 4, 1862.

Here, the breech block is screwed to the top of the stock and swings out to the right. It carries a percussion cap lock with horizontal hammer. Christopher M. Spencer patented this Feb. 4, 1862. It is number 34,319.

the cartridge anvil prevents the use of an effective rear sight.

Another Frenchman, however, came through with a development that completely revolutionized multifire arms. This was the rimfire cartridge designed by Flobert of Paris about 1840. His cartridge, known as the B-B cap was the forerunner of the first successful American rimfire cartridge developed by Smith & Wesson and B. Tyler Henry for the Winchester Repeating Arms Co.

Once the metallic cartridge had reached its fully developed state the day of separate primed guns was gone forever. The breechloader was now as foolproof as the muzzle-loader. One can say that by 1870 all the chief systems of breechloading had been invented. The problem of gas seal having been solved, many systems could now be used. A multitude of actions flowed from the ready hands of inventors. Many resulted from the Civil War, and indeed the majority of breechloaders which various military staffs adopted all over the world were the offerings of American genius. There was the bolt action, the falling block, the dropping block, rolling block, trap door, the tip-down barrel.

It had been during the late years of the Civil War that the United States Military decided to adopt the breechloader. Hitherto the muzzle-loading Springfield had been the arm considered most stalwart by the Army. But its faults could not be glossed over in the face of the smooth breechloaders that were appearing.

By the end of the war, however, there were on hand arsenals full of perfectly good muzzle-loading Springfields. At the same time, money was scarce, and there was no wish to get rid of the huge amount of muzzle-loaders which were in top condition. Would it be possible to convert these arms to breechloaders? Erskine S. Allin, Master Armorer at the Springfield Armory came up with an answer. Conversions started in 1865. Ultimately, and with some minor improvements, the system devised by Master Armorer Allin became the famous .45-70 Springfield which was adopted in 1873.

The new Springfield was efficient, strongly-built, and moreover, simple. It had a movable breech block, which had a firing pin, and was hinged at the front end so that it could be flicked up to open the chamber and eject the used cartridge. It

59

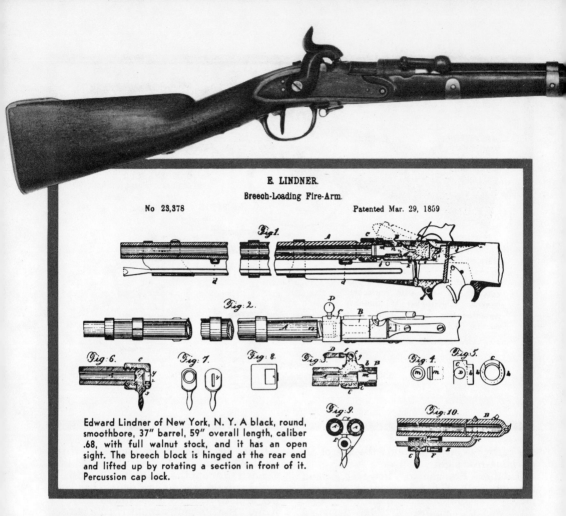

E. LINDNER.

Breech-Loading Fire-Arm.

No 23,378

Patented Mar. 29, 1859

Fig. 1.

Fig. 2.

Fig. 6. *Fig. 7.* *Fig. 8.* *Fig. 3.* *Fig. 4.* *Fig. 5.*

Fig. 9. *Fig. 10.*

Edward Lindner of New York, N. Y. A black, round, smoothbore, 37" barrel, 59" overall length, caliber .68, with full walnut stock, and it has an open sight. The breech block is hinged at the rear end and lifted up by rotating a section in front of it. Percussion cap lock.

was then easy to drop in a new cartridge, snap the block shut, cock the side hammer and be ready to shoot. The weapon used a center-fire cartridge with .45 caliber bullet with 70 grains of black powder.

The Springfield .45-70 served as the chief United States Army rifle and carbine all through the Indian wars, and even as late as World War I some state troops carried the arm.

Great Britain had a similar problem in the changeover from muzzle-loaders to breechloaders. There, too, large supplies of good, solid muzzle-loading rifle-muskets were embarrassingly on hand, and could not be scrapped. In 1865 the British accepted a conversion system by Jacob Snider of New York.

Snider's system also had a hinged breech block, but with the pivot along the side. As with the Springfield there were difficulties in extracting the spent cartridge. But the new Snider-Enfield with Boxer's center-

fire cartridge was found highly efficient.

Amongst the breech systems developed at the close of the Civil War one stood out as the most widely used of all. This was the Remington rolling block. Joseph Rider and Leonard Geiger were the authors of the system at the Remington plant at Ilion, New York. They were greeted by success after their experimentation in April 1865.

The rolling block breech was simple. The breech was opened by the cocking of the hammer and rolling the solid breech block straight back. This could be accomplished by the shooter's thumb. A cartridge was then placed inside and the block rolled back up. A locking lever held the hammer cocked, then locked the breech shut. When the arm was fired the hammer hit the firing pin which was mounted in the breech block and this added its own weight to the breech at the very instant explosion took place. It is said that it was just impossible to blow out a Remington breech.

60

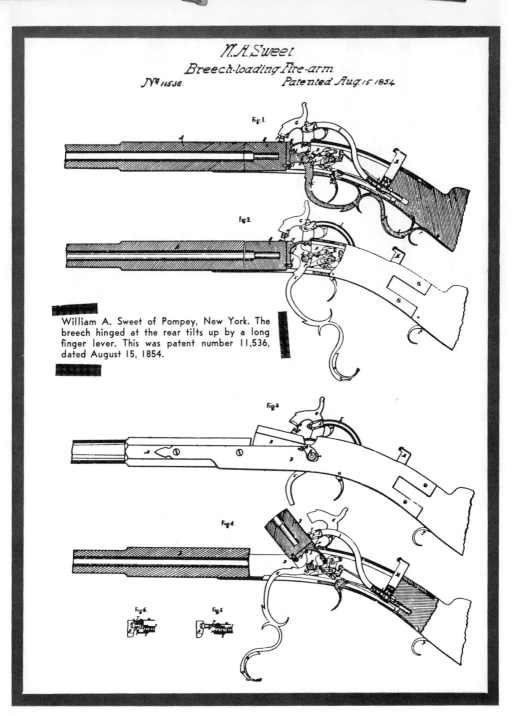

W. A. Sweet
Breech-loading Fire-arm.
Nº 11536. *Patented Aug. 15. 1854*

Fig. 1

Fig. 2

William A. Sweet of Pompey, New York. The breech hinged at the rear tilts up by a long finger lever. This was patent number 11,536, dated August 15, 1854.

Fig. 3

Fig. 4

Fig. 6 Fig. 5

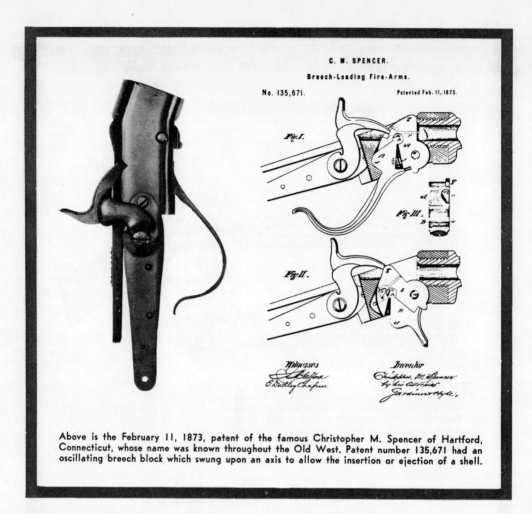

C. M. SPENCER.

Breech-Loading Fire-Arms.

No. 135,671.   Patented Feb. 11, 1873.

Fig.I.

Fig.III.

Fig.II.

Witnesses

Inventor

Above is the February 11, 1873, patent of the famous Christopher M. Spencer of Hartford, Connecticut, whose name was known throughout the Old West. Patent number 135,671 had an oscillating breech block which swung upon an axis to allow the insertion or ejection of a shell.

The Remington rolling block sporting rifle, Model 1866, which was known as the Model No. 1 was considered to be one of the most accurate of the single shot sporting rifles of that time. Later, when it was chambered for a .44-90 cartridge with a 400-grain bullet, the rifle became known as the Remington Buffalo Gun.

Indeed General George Armstrong Custer wrote to Remington in 1873 and told how he had dropped 41 antelope with one of the rolling block .50 caliber Remingtons at an average range of 250 yards.

One of the greatest proofs of the efficacy of the Remington rolling block and its smooth loading and firing characteristics was the fantastic saga of Nelson Story who, with thirty cowhands, assembled 3,000 head of Texas cattle and headed north for the lush grasslands of Montana. Story's cowboys were armed with Remington rolling

block rifles and government issued brass center-fire cartridges. All the way to Wyoming Story and his little band encountered no great difficulty. At Fort Kearney, at that time the nation's most remote Army outpost, the officer in charge, Colonel H. B. Carrington, forbade Story and his men to go any further. According to report, 3,000 Cheyenne and Sioux under command of Red Cloud and Crazy Horse were on the Bozeman Trail which Story and his cowhands planned to follow through into Montana. For two weeks Story and his men waited for Carrington to reconsider and give them permission to pass along the trail, or even for the Colonel to send some cavalry along with them for protection. But Carrington did neither one nor the other. At last, Story and his men broke camp, and without Carrington's permission, headed for Montana on their own.

Charles A. King of Meriden, Connecticut. A double barrel, breech-loading arm with stock and barrel cut off. Overall length of this shotgun is 12 inches. King's invention dealt with that class of breechloading firearms in which the barrel tilts upward at the rear end to expose the chamber for loading and to extract the shells. The object of his invention was to facilitate the separation of the barrel from the frame, and also to relieve the hinge from the dropping of the forward end of the barrels when tilted.

In the meantime, Red Cloud's scouts had reported to their chief that the white men were in the vicinity with a tempting herd of 3,000 longhorns, and that moreover, these were poorly protected. On the afternoon of October 29, 1866, Story and his men spotted Crazy Horse and 500 of his braves riding the ridges high above the valley through which they were progressing. Story assembled his little band of cowpokes in the customary protective wagon train circle as drum beats on the hill tops, signal fires and flashing signals of mirrors suddenly ceased. There were a few moments of silence, then the hordes of Indian warriors raced down the slopes. Story gave the order to open fire. An advance phalanx of charging Indians were driven forever from their ponies and, as it is said in the time-honored western, "bit the dust." Forthwith, the main Indian force closed in, taking advantage—

so they thought—of the accustomed moment of reloading. But they rued that decision. The swift, smooth action of the Remington rolling block never presented a break in the cowboys' withering fire.

The gun barrels of Story's men grew red hot as the .50-70 slugs thudded without letup into the attacking braves and their ponies. Crazy Horse had made a desperate mistake. He had planned his tactics based on the slow muzzle-loading characteristics of the Springfield and its lesser range. His tactical error was fatal to the attacking braves whose estimated 500-strong force was literally cut in half before Crazy Horse and the survivors retired to the hills.

Story continued his slow plodding journey toward the virgin grazing land of Montana. Despite two more brisk attacks by the Indians, he ultimately brought his herd to Galatin, losing only one man to the three

C. SHARPS.

Breech-Loading Fire-Arm.

No. 5,763.   Patented Sept. 12, 1848.

Number 5,763 patented September 12, 1848, by Christian Sharps. Round, smoothbore, 32" barrel, caliber .56, 49 inches overall length, walnut stock. This has two brass bands, an iron ramrod, brass trim. There is a patch box on the side of the stock. The breech block slides downward by operation of a long finger lever. Percussion cap lock, and fixed front and rear sights.

Indian encounters. By contrast, Colonel Carrington's troops, nearly 300 in number, were ignominiously bottled up behind the stockade at Fort Kearney for three days during an attack by the redoubtable Red Cloud. Later, when the redmen had withdrawn Carrington dispatched a scouting unit of troops to report on their disposition. The enterprising Sioux attacked the reconnoitering soldiers and wiped out the entire detachment. Carrington's men were armed with Springfield muzzle-loaders.

Along with a number of other gun manufacturers, Eli Whitney, Jr., and his company, realized that after the end of the Civil War the demand for the now archaic muzzle-loader was swiftly coming to an end. In 1864 Whitney patented a swinging breech. Among Whitney's approved claims was an "exposed breech for receiving the charge . . . tightly closed by giving a horizontal (or nearly so) lateral swinging movement to a pivoted breech-check which has no end-wise play."

This invention included an arrangement whereby the breech piece pivoted from the forward end away from the barrel in substantially the same plane as the barrel. Although the notion was unique, much of its strength depended upon a single anchoring pivot bolt, and this particular Whitney patent never developed beyond the prototype stage.

All the same, Whitney looked with jealousy upon the sale of the Remington rolling block which was one of the most successful single shot breechloaders ever put on the market. The record indicates that at one time Remington produced as many as 1500 of these arms in a day.

In an effort to compete with Remington, Whitney acquired manufacturing rights to

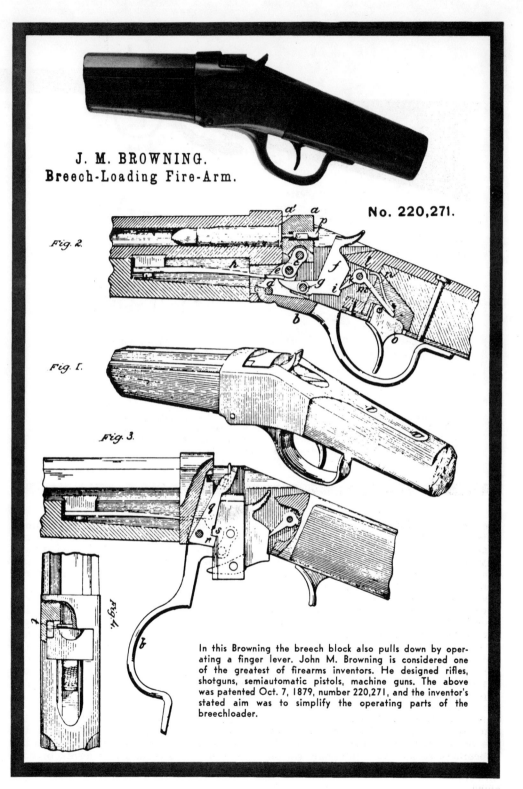

J. M. BROWNING.
Breech-Loading Fire-Arm.

No. 220,271.

Fig. 2.

Fig. 1.

Fig. 3.

Fig. 4.

In this Browning the breech block also pulls down by operating a finger lever. John M. Browning is considered one of the greatest of firearms inventors. He designed rifles, shotguns, semiautomatic pistols, machine guns. The above was patented Oct. 7, 1879, number 220,271, and the inventor's stated aim was to simplify the operating parts of the breechloader.

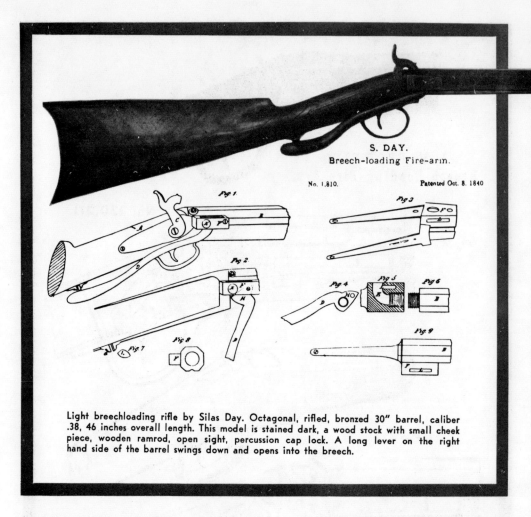

S. DAY.
Breech-loading Fire-arm.

No. 1,810.

Patented Oct. 8. 1840

Light breechloading rifle by Silas Day. Octagonal, rifled, bronzed 30" barrel, caliber .38, 46 inches overall length. This model is stained dark, a wood stock with small cheek piece, wooden ramrod, open sight, percussion cap lock. A long lever on the right hand side of the barrel swings down and opens into the breech.

the Laidley and Emery breechloading patents. The breech piece on the Laidley-Emery patent arm, as improved by Whitney, is of a type that turns down to the rear to open the breech for placing a cartridge. Basically, this was the same as the Remington-Rider design. The real difference was in the means of supporting the breech block during firing. The Whitney breech piece was locked against the rear of the barrel by a cam which drops into position on the rear of the breech block. Because of the way it looks, the mechanism has often raised the notion that this is a superposed loaded firearm with two hammers. Actually, the hammer is an integral part of the swing-back type breech block. The separate cam used to close and lock the breech had a superficial sameness in appearance because of a thumbing ear on the top of the cam.

It was simple to operate the Whitney breechloader. You could do it with one hand. The weapon could be loaded at half-cock because in that position the hammer was secured in a safety notch thus preventing accidental discharge.

This system, although it was in a way similar to Remington's in appearance and a great deal the same in the way it operated, escaped infringement of the Remington-Rider patent because of a difference in extractor design and the cam breech block support. These Whitney firearms are found in either .45 caliber or in military form in a .50 caliber made for the Army and a .44 caliber for the Navy.

Another method of Whitney's with the single shot breechloader was to operate the lock in a side swinging motion across the base of the breech. The Phoenix breechloading rifle that Whitney manufactured

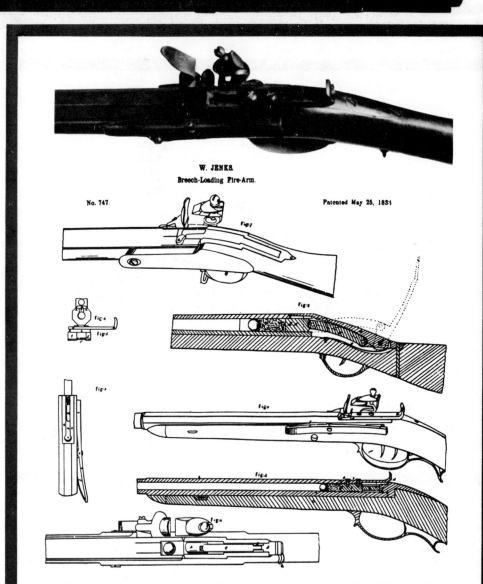

W. JENKS.
Breech-Loading Fire-Arm.

No. 747.

Patented May 25, 1838.

Fig.1

Fig.2

Fig.4

Fig.5

Fig.3

Fig.3

Fig.4

Fig.5

William Jenks of Columbia, South Carolina. Patent number 747, May 25, 1838. Flint-lock breechloader, bronzed, 34" barrel, 51" overall, caliber .36. The walnut stock is made in two pieces, with iron trim. It has two triggers. When the arm is loaded, the stop, which fills the space between the plug and the breech pin, is removed from behind the plug, and the slide is withdrawn. The ball is then dropped in at the opening, and by depressing the muzzle, it rolls forward to the end of the chamber. A charge of powder is then poured in and the slide forced forward.

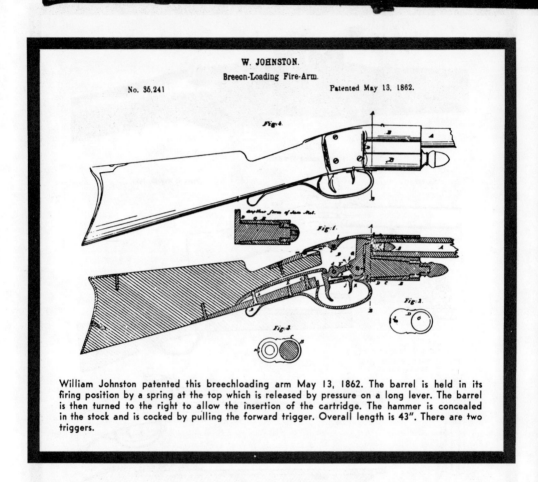

W. JOHNSTON.
Breech-Loading Fire-Arm.

No. 35,241

Patented May 13, 1862.

Fig.4.

another form of Item-Rest.

Fig.1.

Fig.2.

Fig.3.

William Johnston patented this breechloading arm May 13, 1862. The barrel is held in its firing position by a spring at the top which is released by pressure on a long lever. The barrel is then turned to the right to allow the insertion of the cartridge. The hammer is concealed in the stock and is cocked by pulling the forward trigger. Overall length is 43". There are two triggers.

was typical of this type and the Phoenix design was developed from Whitney's dormant 1864 patent. The breech block was hung to one side of the frame and was pivoted transversely to open or close the breech. The basic weakness of this system was the need to swing the breech block mechanism across the base of the shell, with the frustration of being unable to close the breech, if a shell was not firmly seated. The approaching edge of the Phoenix breech block was chamfered on the front side so that as the breech block was closed, this beveled surface was presumed to act as a cam to force the cartridge to properly seat. Sometimes it did, but more often it did not.

The Phoenix rifle, though, had fewer parts than any other breechloading rifle of the time. The mechanism was operated by bringing the hammer back to half cock which permitted the breech block to be swung up to the right. A lever operated by the breech block movement allowed mechanical extraction. But this extracting system proved to be a weakness in the earliest models. The 1872 versions were improved two years later so that the arm was accepted in general as an effective one.

Amongst the great galaxy of firearms in-

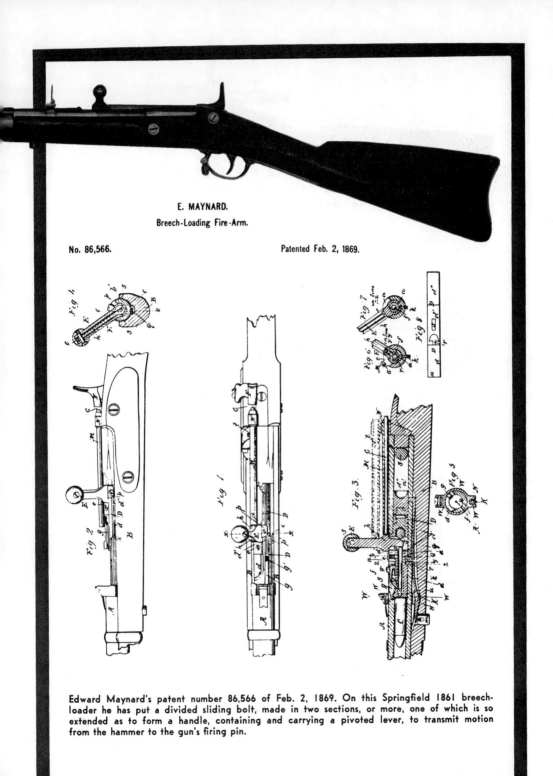

E. MAYNARD.
Breech-Loading Fire-Arm.

No. 86,566.

Patented Feb. 2, 1869.

Edward Maynard's patent number 86,566 of Feb. 2, 1869. On this Springfield 1861 breech-loader he has put a divided sliding bolt, made in two sections, or more, one of which is so extended as to form a handle, containing and carrying a pivoted lever, to transmit motion from the hammer to the gun's firing pin.

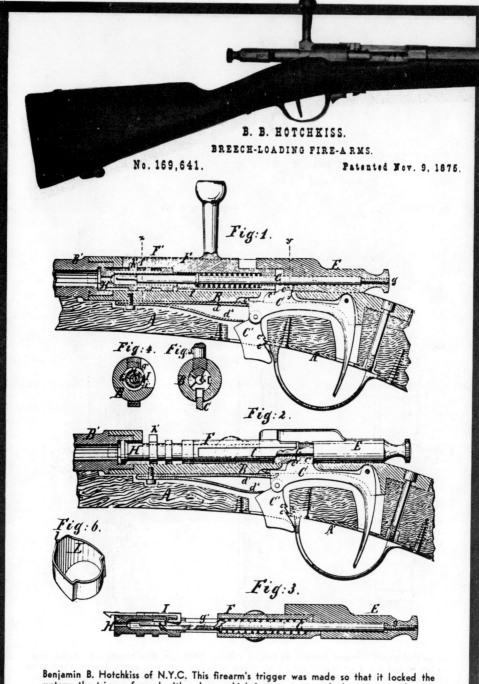

B. B. HOTCHKISS.
BREECH-LOADING FIRE-ARMS.

No. 169,641.

Patented Nov. 9, 1875.

Fig:1.

Fig:4. Fig:5.

Fig:2.

Fig:6.

Fig:3.

Benjamin B. Hotchkiss of N.Y.C. This firearm's trigger was made so that it locked the system; the trigger formed with a lever which in turn was notched to prevent the gun from accidentally firing. Number 169,641. Bolt lock mechanism. Iron ramrod, iron trim, 52 inches overall length.

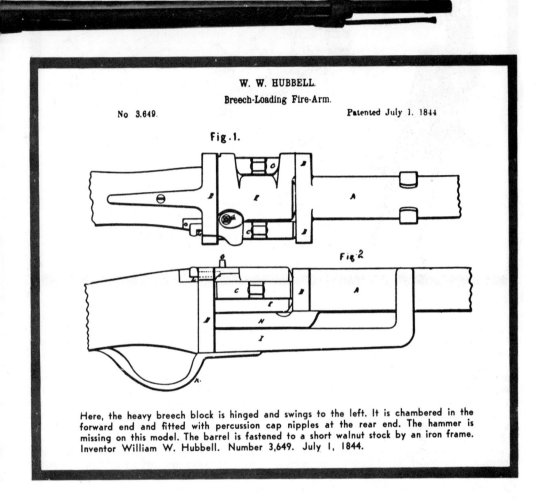

W. W. HUBBELL.

Breech-Loading Fire-Arm.

No 3,649.

Patented July 1, 1844

Fig.1.

Fig.2

Here, the heavy breech block is hinged and swings to the left. It is chambered in the forward end and fitted with percussion cap nipples at the rear end. The hammer is missing on this model. The barrel is fastened to a short walnut stock by an iron frame. Inventor William W. Hubbell. Number 3,649. July 1, 1844.

ventors one must by no means overlook that remarkable man Christian M. Spencer. Spencer was twenty-seven years old when he was granted a patent for a movable breech rolling block action repeating firearm with tubular magazine in the butt. One can well argue the point that even though the birth of the repeating rifle is most accurately traced back to the Hunt and Jennings inventions in 1849, much, much credit must be given to Spencer.

The Spencer was a finger lever action, utilizing the trigger guard to operate the seven-shot repeater. In the beginning, the Spencer cartridges were loaded slowly, one at a time, through a trap in the butt plate. Later, the arm was improved by the intro-

duction of the Blakelee Cartridge Box, a handy speed-up loading item that included ten seven-shot tubes. The Blakelee tubes funneled the cartridges into the Spencer magazine in a single, easy, one-handed motion.

At the outset of the Civil War Spencer was unable to get Army officials to test his rifle. Finally, he went directly to President Lincoln. Apparently, Lincoln tested the rifle himself on the Capitol grounds and was so impressed that he gave the young inventor an order for 10,000 of the arms right then and there.

The Spencer, both rifle and carbine versions, were later considered highly by United States Army Ordnance. Eventually

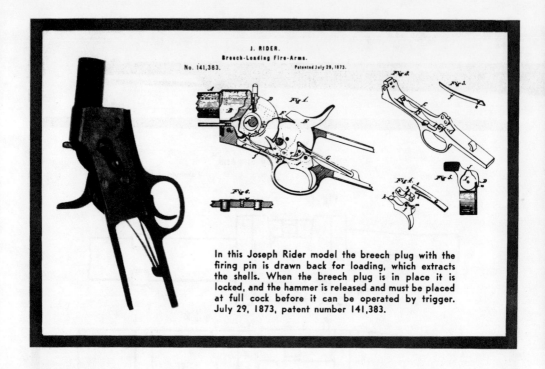

J. RIDER.
Breech-Loading Fire-Arms.
No. 141,383.
Patented July 29, 1873.

In this Joseph Rider model the breech plug with the firing pin is drawn back for loading, which extracts the shells. When the breech plug is in place it is locked, and the hammer is released and must be placed at full cock before it can be operated by trigger. July 29, 1873, patent number 141,383.

the government bought approximately 94,000 Spencers.

At first the Spencer could only be used as a repeater. Yet, the majority of government issue models had a cut-off feature so that the weapon could be loaded and fired as a single-shot breechloader. E. M. Stabler invented this feature, and it appeared on all Spencers manufactured after 1866.

Most of the Civil War Spencers were made under contract by the Burnside Rifle Company, Providence, R.I., for Spencer. As a result of this there has occasionally appeared historical reference to the Spencer as the Burnside. The majority of the Civil War Spencers were .52 caliber, using what was called the No. 56 Spencer rimfire cartridge, which was later called the Spencer .56-56.

The Army or Navy versions of the rifle ranged from $38 to $43. The cartridges cost $25 a thousand. War contracts to Spencer amounted to more than five million dollars.

After the war Spencer brought out a sporting rifle in .44 caliber which used the No. 46 Spencer cartridge, commonly known as the .56-46 Spencer. Spencers were made with three and six groove rifling, although the latter was more common. At the end of the Civil War Spencer lost control, it appears, of the Spencer Repeating Rifle Company. Spencer worked with other partners for a while. On September 12, 1869, the Spencer Repeating Rifle Company ceased production. The company was bought by Winchester.

One of the problems, of course, had been black powder. Black powder had always had the unfortunate drawback of fouling rifle bores. In many cases, too, it did not exactly help the clarity of one's vision, say, in a close passage at arms with some desperate adversary. Its uneven burning characteristics also produced low velocities which necessitated reliance upon heavy projectiles to be effective.

Following the preliminary work of Christian Shoebein, Ascanio Subero, and Nobel, a French chemist named Paul Vieille created smokeless powder. The basis of Vieille's smokeless powder was a mixture of cellulose nitrates, which was called pyroxylin, treated with camphor. This, as a matter of fact, had been used for years in men's collars and was called celluloid. The celluloid when dissolved in ether or alcohol produced a compound that could be dried and used instead of black powder. This was called Poudre B.

Poudre B, and its more refined smokeless successors, was neither in powder form, nor was it smokeless, but it did have far lesser fouling effects than did black powder. It imparted a far greater pressure rise

The famous Eliphalet Remington. Rider worked closely with Remington, a name which, like Colt and Deringer, is part of our history.

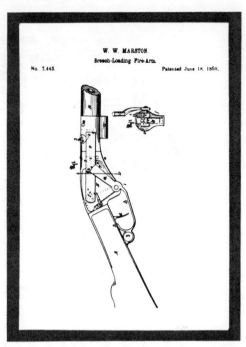

W. W. Marston's arm has finger lever which forms part of trigger guard; operates breech block which slides back from end of barrel. No. 7,443.

At right, B. Tyler Henry, another fabulous man of firearms who was the very backbone of the Winchester Arms Company.

upon ignition than did the black powder.

Smokeless powder's arrival on the scene required, of course, a more rigid analysis of the alloy and molecular structure of metals to prevent the commonplace early occurrences in smokeless powder cartridge manufacturing, "cutoffs," that is splits, ruptures and swelling of the cases as a consequence of inconsistent strength characteristics of the brass which was used. It goes without saying that the effort in this direction was successful.

Within the short span of one hundred years, gun development had moved from flint and percussion ignition systems to modern breechloading repeating rifles using self-contained metal cartridges and with the turn of the century, gunmakers' products were built to handle the new high velocity smokeless powder ammunition. By 1900 the gun had progressed from the heavy matchlock to the sleek, handy weapon of Spencer, Remington and the others. But more was to come. ■

THE REVOLVING CYLINDER

Without question the revolver is, and always has been, a dramatic weapon. It is fast, it has power, and it moves; it is therefore highly appealing in that so much in the way of action is associated with it. By definition, it is a gun with a number of barrels, or a cylinder with several chambers that turns around a central point. It can therefore be a pistol or a shoulder arm; or a machine gun. It is as a handgun that we think of it, however.

A GOOD MANY SCHOLARS assert that Captain Artemus Wheeler, the Yankee experimenter in firearms, should receive the credit for developing the revolver; or at any rate that his successor, Elisha Hayden Collier of Boston, Massachusetts should receive the honor. Collier did in fact design a successful single-barreled repeating firearm with hand-turned cylinder. He applied for a patent, the arm having been invented and developed in Boston during the first ten years of the 19th century. The patent was finally granted in England in 1818.

It is difficult to say whether those who give credit to Collier are purists or are simply trying to detract from the vast acknowledgement given Sam Colt. It is true that chronologically Collier did precede Colt, but it was in fact Colt who did produce the first practical and *mechanically* operated *percussion* type revolving cylinder multishot weapon.

There is no question that other inventors had taken up Shaw's percussion cap idea and were at work applying the new principle to multishot weapons, some prior to Colt, others at the same time.

On April 13, 1836, the brothers Barton and Benjamin Darling of Bellingham, Massachusetts, patented a rotary pistol or revolver. The first model of their patented arm was a six-shot of the pepperbox type. The pepperbox consists of a cluster of three or more barrels. Its basic difference from a revolver is that the pepperbox has revolving barrels, while the revolver has a revolving cylinder with all shots passing through a single barrel.

Firearms designers had patented side-by-side, double barreled pill locks with Forsyth type mechanisms, percussion double barrels with side-by-side or over-and-under configuration with Shaw-type percussion cap mechanisms before 1830, but Sam Colt's patent of February 25, 1836, in time sequence nearly two months ahead of the Darling brothers, laid proper claim to a mechanically rotated percussion type repeater.

It can no longer be proved why it was that similar patents were granted to both Colt and the Darlings, or even if they were actually granted. Within one year after the Colt and Darling developments the United States Patent Office burned, and in the fire went whatever "evidence" there may have been.

Benjamin Darling, who died near the end of the century, insisted that his was the first American revolver. The cool fact is that Colt's approach was the more practical and the one destined to gain vast approval and acceptance by the gun-buying public. Darling's revolving pepperbox approach to repeating percussion firearms was to have a brief 20-year period of acceptance. After that time, the Darling and its imitators' or licensees' products were to become relegated to curiosity items.

Colt's first model, referred to as the Paterson Colt, a 5-shot folding trigger 9½" long, .34 caliber arm with a 5½" octagonal barrel, was not a great commercial success at the start. Yet its features incorporated those which basically were to be a part of the Colts that were produced throughout the whole of the percussion period.

One of the most important features that was covered by Sam Colt's patent was the mechanically operated cylinder. At the same time, there were other very essential features that were also a part of Colt's design.

It was Samuel Colt who placed the percussion cones on the rear of the loading chambers rather than on the top, and he separated each cone with a metal barrier in order to prevent chain ignition. He also developed a method to mechanically lock the cylinder mechanism in order to insure relatively exact alignment of the chamber that was to be fired with the barrel.

To be sure, the principle of the revolving type breech had been used in each progressive period in firearms development. Many other inventors during the early percussion era worked along similar lines.

Indeed, revolving firearms had appeared before the end of the 16th century. There is, for instance, a matchlock pistol with three revolving barrels, in Venice which, it is claimed, is the same as one listed in a city inventory dated 1548. There are other examples of early revolvers in other parts of the world.

There were, to be sure, problems in developing a true revolver. It goes without saying that the cylinder had to revolve easily, and it also had to line up precisely with the barrel breech and also lock tightly in that position while the arm was fired. If it didn't, then the power of the charge could drive the bullet into the frame or side of the barrel with unfortunate results for both the weapon and the shooter's hand.

One interesting suggestion came from an English gunsmith named James Gorgo, in the late 17th century. Foregoing the effort to line up the breech and chamber, Gorgo tried a funnel to catch the bullet and deflect it into the barrel. Although this was

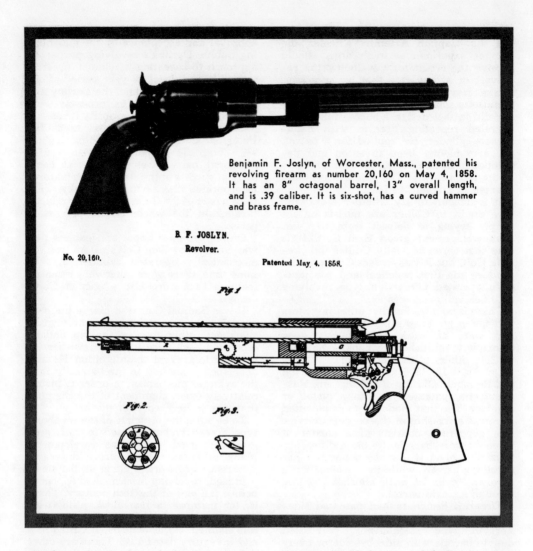

Benjamin F. Joslyn, of Worcester, Mass., patented his revolving firearm as number 20,160 on May 4, 1858. It has an 8" octagonal barrel, 13" overall length, and is .39 caliber. It is six-shot, has a curved hammer and brass frame.

B. F. JOSLYN.
Revolver.

No. 20,160.

Patented May 4. 1858.

Fig. 1

Fig. 2.

Fig. 3.

an obviously simple and also inexpensive idea, it was not really practical.

However, a contemporary of Gorgo's came up with a better idea. James Puckle, in 1718, patented a revolver, a large one about the size of a wall gun, and it was mounted on a tripod. This unique weapon had a barrel and interchangeable cylinders with a variety of charges. The cylinders were turned by hand. A crank at the back was used to tighten them against the barrel for each discharge, and there was a fairly tight joint at the mouth of each chamber, shaped like a cone where it fitted into the breech and helped solve the problem of escaping gas. The arm could be fired either by flintlock or match. The inventor was quite a salesman, and he announced with considerable pride, it appears, that his

weapon could fire round bullets against Christians and square bullets against Turks. He provided special cylinders for whatever the occasion demanded. Puckle had trouble marketing his gun. It was almost a century later that Captain Artemus Wheeler obtained his patent for a ". . . gun to discharge 7 or more times," on June 10, 1818. The arm was a flintlock revolver priming magazine. Wheeler failed to interest the Navy in his weapon and it appears he did not push his invention after this.

Following Colt, Nichols and Childs of Conway, Massachusetts, patented, on April 24, 1838, a percussion revolver with a manually revolved cylinder and a revolving rifle. Their cylinder gas seal was not tight, however.

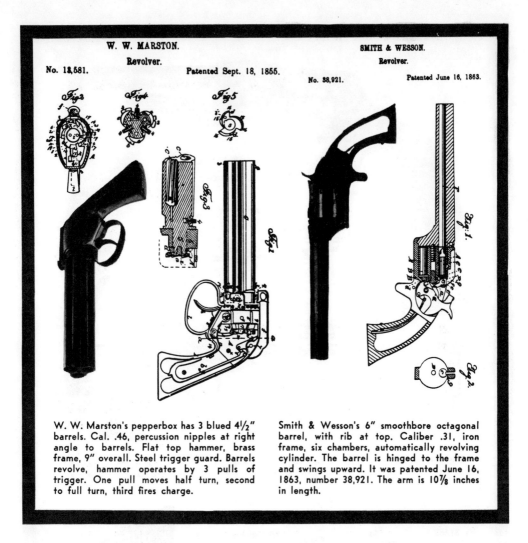

W. W. MARSTON.
Revolver.

No. 13,581.

Patented Sept. 18, 1855.

SMITH & WESSON.
Revolver.

No. 38,921.

Patented June 16, 1863.

W. W. Marston's pepperbox has 3 blued 4½″ barrels. Cal. .46, percussion nipples at right angle to barrels. Flat top hammer, brass frame, 9″ overall. Steel trigger guard. Barrels revolve, hammer operates by 3 pulls of trigger. One pull moves half turn, second to full turn, third fires charge.

Smith & Wesson's 6″ smoothbore octagonal barrel, with rib at top. Caliber .31, iron frame, six chambers, automatically revolving cylinder. The barrel is hinged to the frame and swings upward. It was patented June 16, 1863, number 38,921. The arm is 10⅞ inches in length.

We have already mentioned the work of John Webster Cochran who, working separately and uninfluenced by Colt was issued a patent on April 28, 1837, for a horizontally revolving, underhammer type repeater usually referred to as a monitor or turret gun. Cochran turret guns were made in both rifle and pistol form, in five, seven, and eight-shot versions. Other similar monitor-type arms were made under Cochran's patent by other gun manufacturers. The cylinder was turned by hand and although the guns were rather unwieldy, collectors' specimens today are still frequently in good firing condition for the reason that the mechanism was solidly built, uncomplicated, and also easy to maintain.

The far less practical Porter with a vertically rotated cylinder was a variation of the Cochran turret type arm. The Porter was introduced initially in hand revolving form, as an 8-shot, .36 caliber with a tape lock.

Later, the designer, Patrick W. Porter of New York City, patented another version using a pill lock. This one was a .50 caliber rifle with a 28″ octagonal barrel. Unhappily for Mr. Porter, one of his firearms backfired while he was demonstrating it to Colonel Colt and some others. Despite a steel protective covering fitted to the vertical cylinder, Porter was mortally wounded.

Some time later, George Foster of Taunton, Massachusetts, who had made the original model that killed its inventor, collected miscellaneous parts and as-

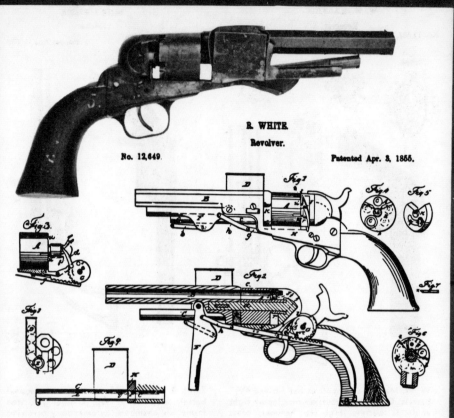

R. WHITE

Revolver.

No. 12,649.

Patented Apr. 3, 1855.

Rollin White has combined the hammer with the charging piston so that in the operation of moving the charging piston to drive cartridge from magazine, the hammer is raised to cock the lock.

R. WHITE.

Revolving Fire-Arm.

No. 93,653.

Patented Aug. 10, 1869.

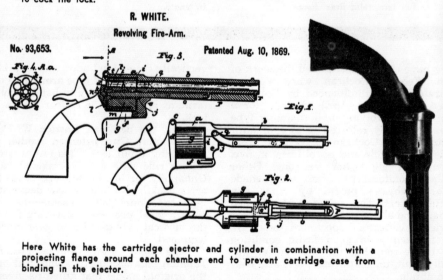

Here White has the cartridge ejector and cylinder in combination with a projecting flange around each chamber end to prevent cartridge case from binding in the ejector.

R. WHITE.

Revolver.

No. 19,961.

Patented Apr. 13, 1858.

Octagonal, rifled 3½" barrel, caliber .32, 8" overall length, 5-chambered automatic revolving cylinder, revolves to left. Flat top hammer, separate ring behind cylinder with percussion channels. Another Rollin White. Number 19,961, dated April 13, 1858.

sembled them at Providence, R. I. For a number of years these Porter revolving arms were sold in small quantities, and today they are desirable collectors' items.

It was Ethan Allen who improved on the Darling pepperboxes with a double-action feature so that pulling the trigger not only cocked but fired his multishot revolving cluster barrels. A decided advantage here was the rapidity of fire, although like the others, the Allen pepperbox was subject to gas blow-back and chain-fire.

Although Colonel Sam Colt manufactured revolving percussion rifles in 1837, they were for these very reasons not popular. Yet in October, 1837, the American Institute of the city of New York for the Encouragement of Science and Invention presented Colt with a gold medal in recognition of his multichambered cylinder rifle. It is reported that Colt had been able to load with powder and ball and prime with percussion caps a ten-chambered rifle, getting off fifty shots in eight minutes and forty-five seconds. According to report, of forty shots fired at a 12-by-30-inch target at a distance of forty yards, twenty-three struck the target.

The enterprising Eli Whitney also produced a large number of revolvers. Beginning with a hand-rotated, brass framed, caliber .28, 4" octagonal-barreled 5-shot arm in the late thirties, he continued with two double trigger models, both of the hand-rotated cylinder type in the late 1840s, a ring trigger model in 1854 and the Whitney-Beal, another ring trigger type later that same year.

In any event, the Darlings' is the first American patent for a pepperbox. It is surmised by some experts that the same system reached popularity in Europe at the same time. These were single-action pistols. In other words, one had to pull the hammer back in order to cock the gun and rotate the barrels before firing a shot.

It was not long before the next step eliminated this procedure. Now came the gun that cocked itself, the double-action. One pull of the trigger cocked the hammer, turned the barrels, and fired the weapon. It has been pointed out that because of the

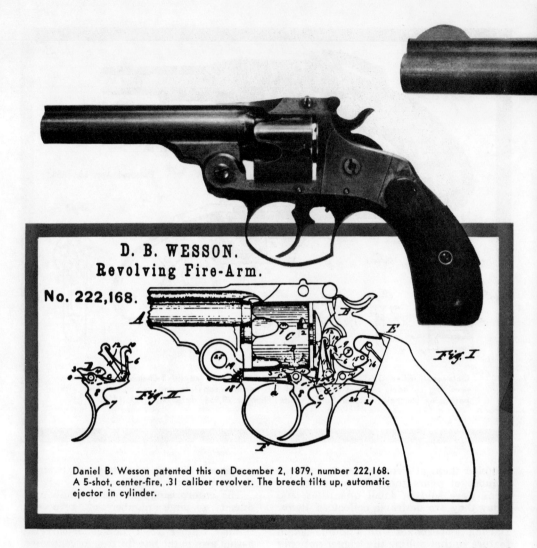

D. B. WESSON.
Revolving Fire-Arm.

No. 222,168.

Daniel B. Wesson patented this on December 2, 1879, number 222,168. A 5-shot, center-fire, .31 caliber revolver. The breech tilts up, automatic ejector in cylinder.

fact that the idea of the double-action was already known, there is no English patent for a double-action pepperbox. In the United States there had also been no patent on a double-action, and as a consequence Ethan Allen, who incidentally was not the Revolutionary War hero, claimed its invention. This was in 1837. Allen, like Wheeler, Collier, the Darling brothers, was also a true New Englander, from Massachusetts. He moved through a number of partnerships with some of his relatives with the result that he became America's most important pepperbox manufacturer. His arm was the fastest in firing of its time, and for some ten years it was better known and better liked than Sam Colt's.

The pepperbox was really a fast weapon, in double-action that is to say. Loaded and primed in advance it could be whipped out of the pocket and fired in one swift and easy motion. Sometimes the hammers were streamlined, sometimes they were enclosed. There were also numerous barrels, and therefore even a fearful beginner could be reasonably sure of hitting some part of his target if he kept on firing. Most of the models had from four to six barrels, but some models had up to eighteen.

That the pepperbox was popular goes without saying. Homeowners, shopkeepers, bartenders, dancehall girls, gamblers, one and all favored the trusty little weapon. Even the Army used the pepperbox upon occasion.

The gun had its defects, however. To begin with, it was inaccurate. On a number

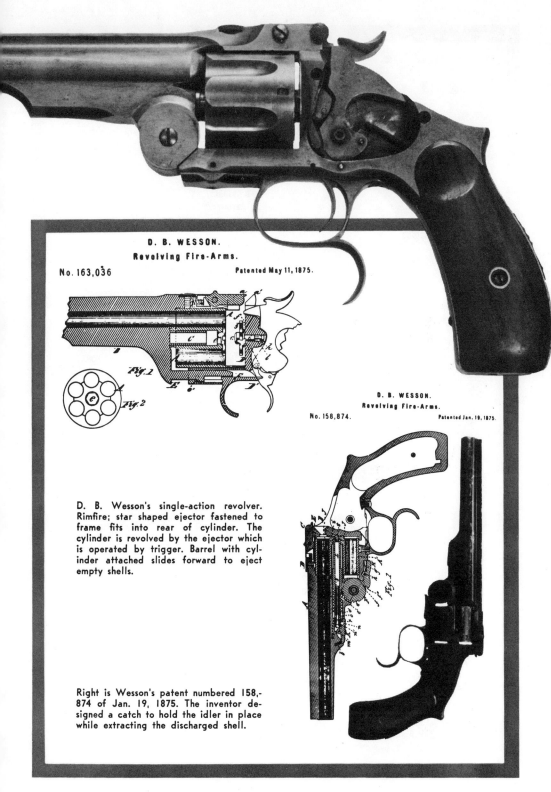

D. B. WESSON.
Revolving Fire-Arms.

No. 163,036   Patented May 11, 1875.

Fig.1

Fig.2

D. B. WESSON.
Revolving Fire-Arms.

No. 158,874.   Patented Jan. 19, 1875.

Fig.1

D. B. Wesson's single-action revolver. Rimfire; star shaped ejector fastened to frame fits into rear of cylinder. The cylinder is revolved by the ejector which is operated by trigger. Barrel with cylinder attached slides forward to eject empty shells.

Right is Wesson's patent numbered 158,-874 of Jan. 19, 1875. The inventor designed a catch to hold the idler in place while extracting the discharged shell.

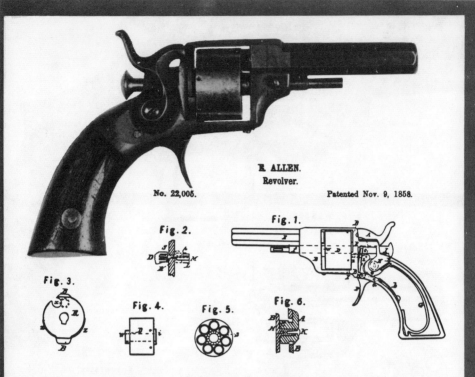

E. ALLEN.
Revolver.

No. 22,005.

Patented Nov. 9, 1858.

Fig. 2.

Fig. 1.

Fig. 3.

Fig. 4.

Fig. 5.

Fig. 6.

Ethan Allen. Single-action revolver, rimfire, no trigger guard, 7-chambered. Allen was given a patent here on a bored-through cylinder. Number 22,005. Nov. 9, 1858.

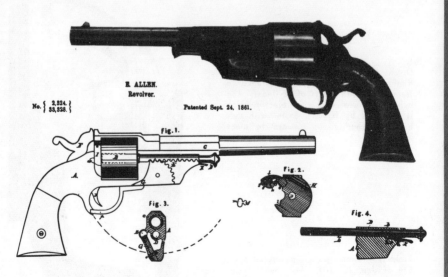

E. ALLEN.
Revolver.

No. { 2,524. }
     { 33,528. }

Patented Sept. 24, 1861.

Fig. 1.

Fig. 2.

Fig. 3.

Fig. 4.

This Allen has a 6-chambered cylinder and is automatically revolved by cocking the hammer. The hinged piece behind cylinder swings upward to allow entry of cartridges.

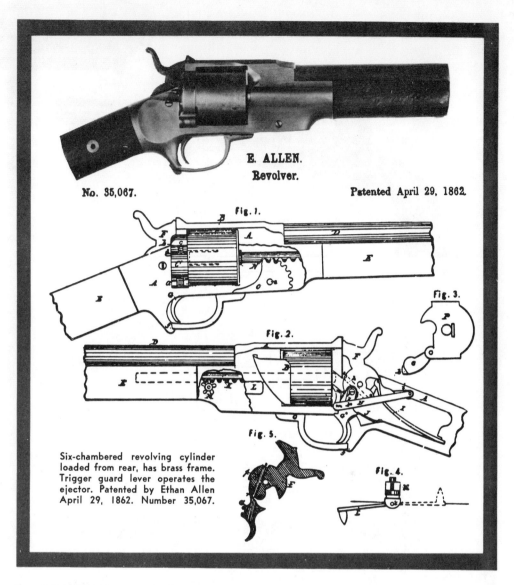

E. ALLEN.
Revolver.

No. 35,067.

Patented April 29, 1862.

Fig. 1.

Fig. 2.

Fig. 3.

Fig. 5.

Fig. 4.

Six-chambered revolving cylinder loaded from rear, has brass frame. Trigger guard lever operates the ejector. Patented by Ethan Allen April 29, 1862. Number 35,067.

of models the hammer got in the way of the shooter's line of vision. The trigger pull was heavy, and the motion of the barrels revolving jarred the gun so that it was hard to maintain one's aim. There was also one other, rude defect, which was that the pepperbox sometimes fired more than one barrel at a time when the flash from one charge spread to another. In general, the gun was clumsy, especially when there were more than eight barrels.

Fortunately, these defects were overcome with the arrival of the percussion revolver. The one barrel settled the extra weight problem, with the result that accurate aiming became a clear possibility.

Although it may be argued that Sam Colt was not legitimately the father of the modern revolver, no one can gainsay his contribution to the popularizing of the handgun. There is no doubt of his authentic place in the history of firearms. And, indeed, he did produce the first practical revolver.

It was not all peaches and cream for young Sam Colt, however. He had difficulty raising money, and after some years Colt finally found himself ready to manufacture his revolver. At his Paterson, N.J., plant he made not only revolving pistols,

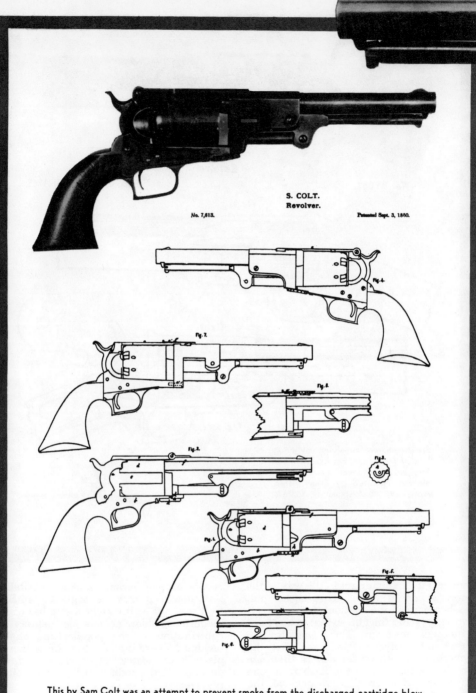

S. COLT.
Revolver.

No. 7,613.   Patented Sept. 3, 1850.

This by Sam Colt was an attempt to prevent smoke from the discharged cartridge blowing into the bore and accumulating dirt to stop the operation of the cylinder. A central opening was bored clear through the cylinder and then the forward end was plugged. The gun is a Model 1848 Dragoon. Patent number 7,613; Sept. 3, 1850.

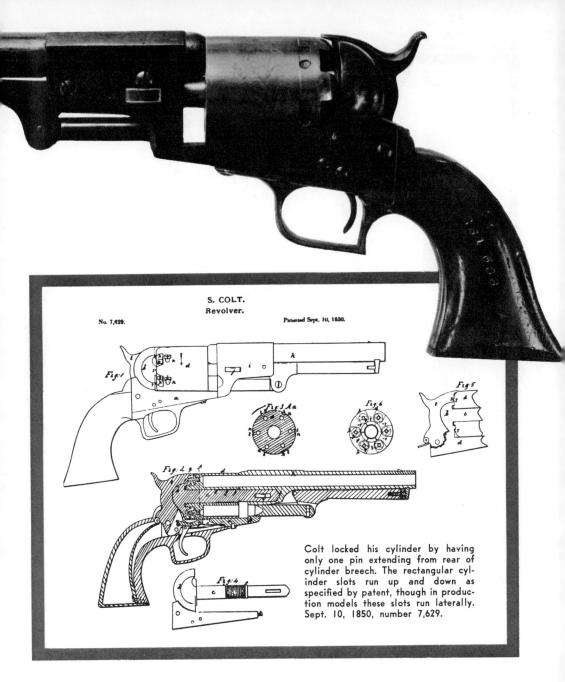

S. COLT.
Revolver.

No. 7,629.

Patented Sept. 10, 1850.

Colt locked his cylinder by having only one pin extending from rear of cylinder breech. The rectangular cylinder slots run up and down as specified by patent, though in production models these slots run laterally. Sept. 10, 1850, number 7,629.

but rifles, shotguns, and carbines. The company failed. The pepperbox was still the big handgun in the civilian market and Colt was unsuccessful in getting a government contract for his arms. In 1843 the Paterson factory shut down.

Then things took a turn for the better. Way out West men had found the new gun useful. In a fight with Indians or outlaws it was second to none. Along the Texas border the arm was finding its way. Famous Texas Ranger Captain Jack Hays swore by the Colt. When the Mexican War broke out the Texas Rangers took part and Captain Samuel H. Walker was sent to find Sam Colt and urge him to go back into gun production. Walker was successful. He also helped redesign the revolver itself. The result was a stronger and more powerful arm. The Walker Colt of 1847 was issued

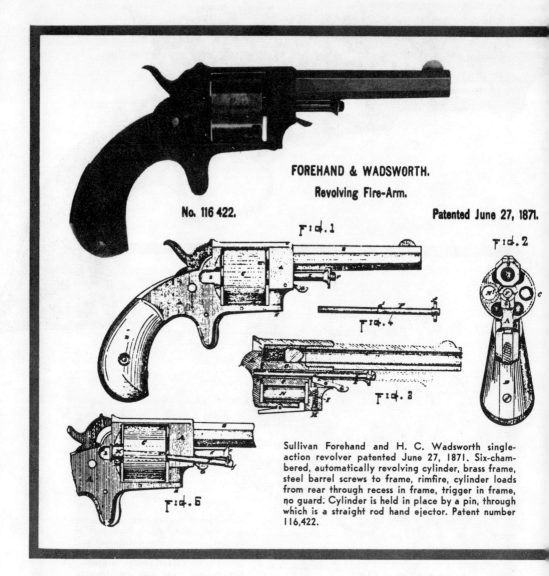

FOREHAND & WADSWORTH.
Revolving Fire-Arm.

No. 116,422.

Patented June 27, 1871.

Sullivan Forehand and H. C. Wadsworth single-action revolver patented June 27, 1871. Six-chambered, automatically revolving cylinder, brass frame, steel barrel screws to frame, rimfire, cylinder loads from rear through recess in frame, trigger in frame, no guard. Cylinder is held in place by a pin, through which is a straight rod hand ejector. Patent number 116,422.

by the Army and the United States became the first nation of the world to issue revolvers to its men. The revolver had finally arrived.

Following the Mexican War the gold rush to California helped enormously in the sale of revolvers. Then the Crimean War brought another rich market for the arm. Swiftly, other companies joined the swim. The Massachusetts Arms Company imitated the Colt and was sued by the Colonel. Remington brought out a handgun with a solid frame, and in fact many modern gun folk feel that it was a better arm than the Colt. Yet, it was not as popular as the Colt in that day. After the

Colt patent ran out and the Civil War started there was an enormous demand for hand arms of the revolver type.

In February 1851 Robert Adams patented a double-action revolver in England. Adams' gun had a solid frame, which he maintained made the gun stronger than any Colt, a bigger bore which afforded greater stopping power. The double-action lock made the weapon a faster firer than the Colt, because with the Colt it was necessary to cock the hammer separately.

On the other hand, the Colt had better accuracy and a greater range. The mechanism was simpler and, very important, the gun was made by machine on a produc-

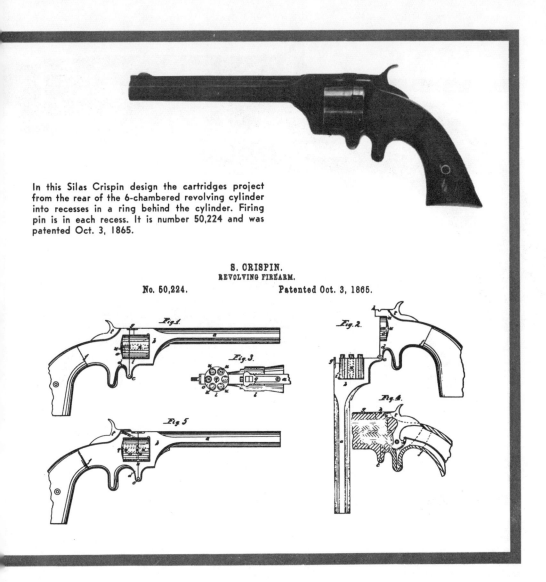

In this Silas Crispin design the cartridges project from the rear of the 6-chambered revolving cylinder into recesses in a ring behind the cylinder. Firing pin is in each recess. It is number 50,224 and was patented Oct. 3, 1865.

S. CRISPIN.
REVOLVING FIREARM.

No. 50,224.

Patented Oct. 3, 1865.

tion line and had interchangeable parts.

A contemporary of Colt who was a man of high imagination, practicality, and enterprise was Dr. Jean Alexandre François Le Mat of New Orleans. Dr. Le Mat patented his ten-shot arm in 1856. It was a redoubtable weapon. The cylinder was bored for nine chambers which fired in the regular manner through a rifled barrel. Le Mat made his gun in .36 and .42 calibers. Right underneath the barrel was another barrel, smoothbore, of .60 caliber which one could load with buckshot and fire by turning down the nose of the hammer. In its day the weapon was nicknamed the grapeshot revolver. Dr. Le Mat claimed,

and with obvious truth, that his weapon was a formidable one.

The Le Mat was also a highly dependable weapon. Although the officers who tested it for the United States Army gave it their highest recommendation, Ordnance was nonetheless not interested. However, with the start of the Civil War the South placed orders quickly and Le Mat went to France to arrange for production of his revolver. Not very long afterwards, blockade runners were bringing the new weapon to southern ports.

The Le Mat lasted past the Civil War, and some models even had the new metallic cartridges, but eventually the

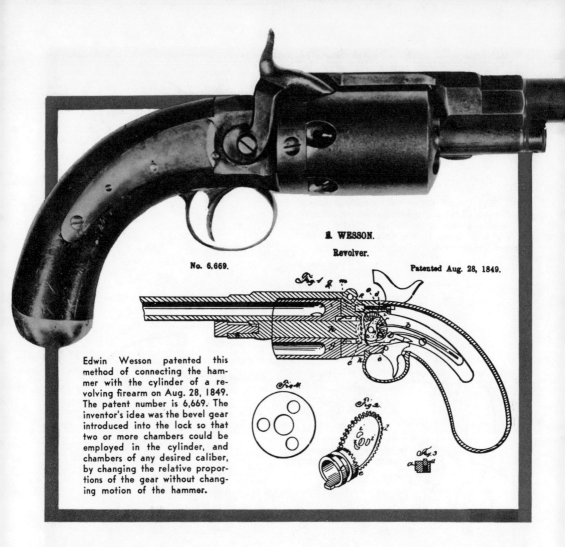

E. WESSON.
Revolver.

No. 6,669.

Patented Aug. 28, 1849.

Edwin Wesson patented this method of connecting the hammer with the cylinder of a revolving firearm on Aug. 28, 1849. The patent number is 6,669. The inventor's idea was the bevel gear introduced into the lock so that two or more chambers could be employed in the cylinder, and chambers of any desired caliber, by changing the relative proportions of the gear without changing motion of the hammer.

company ceased production. The days of the percussion revolver were now heading toward twilight. The metallic cartridge took over. For a number of years revolvers that fired the new ammunition had been developing.

The French tried the new weapons in a big way, using the pin-fire cartridges of Le Faucheux and later Houiller. It was two Americans, however, who made the cartridge revolver something to remember. Both Horace Smith and Daniel B. Wesson had been gunsmiths from their tender years. They had served strict apprenticeships and had worked with various gunmakers in Connecticut. Presently they came together and worked making gun barrels for Allen, Brown & Luther. They developed a friendship and shortly pooled their efforts. In 1851 Smith took out a

patent on a breechloading rifle. Together they designed a repeating magazine rifle and pistol; and then formed a partnership to manufacture their new guns. In 1854 they sold out to the Volcanic Arms Company. Wesson stayed on as factory superintendent, while Smith retired to run a livery stable with a relative.

But the friendship had not died. They had developed an improved rimfire cartridge and they wished to design a revolver that would fire it just as soon as the Colt patent ran out in 1857. They soon designed their gun, but there remained a rather stiff problem. Somebody else had patented a cylinder with the chambers bored through so that a cartridge could be loaded from the breech. In view of the fact that this was an absolutely essential feature for any properly-designed cartridge revolver,

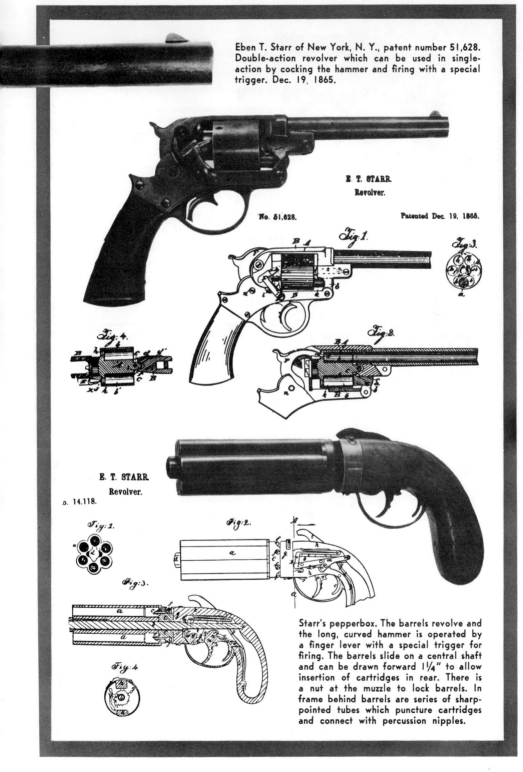

Eben T. Starr of New York, N. Y., patent number 51,628. Double-action revolver which can be used in single-action by cocking the hammer and firing with a special trigger. Dec. 19, 1865.

E. T. STARR.
Revolver.

No. 51,628.   Patented Dec. 19, 1865.

Fig. 1.   Fig. 3.

Fig. 4.   Fig. 2.

E. T. STARR.
Revolver.

p. 14,118.

Fig. 1.   Fig. 2.

Fig. 3.

Fig. 4.

Starr's pepperbox. The barrels revolve and the long, curved hammer is operated by a finger lever with a special trigger for firing. The barrels slide on a central shaft and can be drawn forward 1¼" to allow insertion of cartridges in rear. There is a nut at the muzzle to lock barrels. In frame behind barrels are series of sharp-pointed tubes which puncture cartridges and connect with percussion nipples.

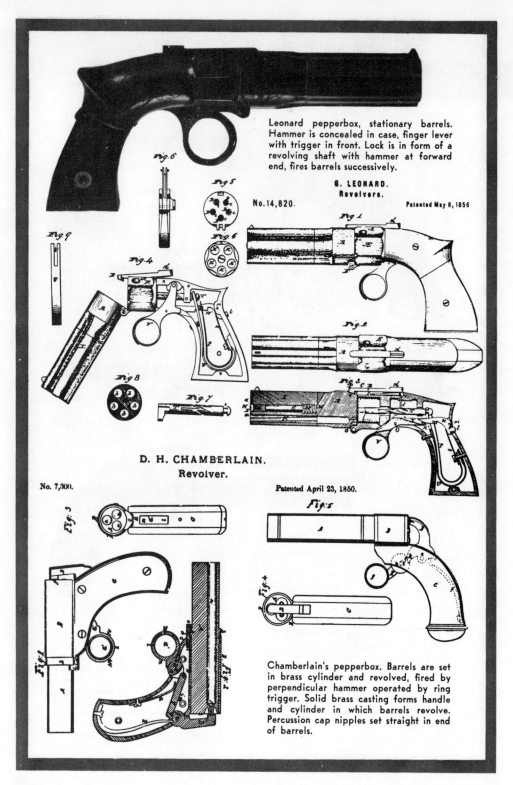

Leonard pepperbox, stationary barrels. Hammer is concealed in case, finger lever with trigger in front. Lock is in form of a revolving shaft with hammer at forward end, fires barrels successively.

G. LEONARD.
Revolvers.

No. 14,820.

Patented May 6, 1856

D. H. CHAMBERLAIN.
Revolver.

No. 7,300.

Patented April 23, 1850

Chamberlain's pepperbox. Barrels are set in brass cylinder and revolved, fired by perpendicular hammer operated by ring trigger. Solid brass casting forms handle and cylinder in which barrels revolve. Percussion cap nipples set straight in end of barrels.

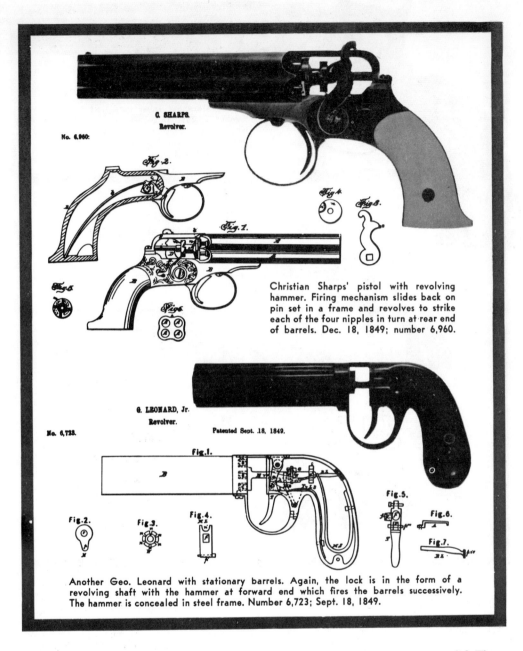

Christian Sharps' pistol with revolving hammer. Firing mechanism slides back on pin set in a frame and revolves to strike each of the four nipples in turn at rear end of barrels. Dec. 18, 1849; number 6,960.

Another Geo. Leonard with stationary barrels. Again, the lock is in the form of a revolving shaft with the hammer at forward end which fires the barrels successively. The hammer is concealed in steel frame. Number 6,723; Sept. 18, 1849.

Smith & Wesson were momentarily stumped. But not for very long. They simply set out to obtain rights to use the new patent. The patent had been granted to Rollin White of New Haven, Connecticut, in 1855. Fortunately for S & W it covered a highly impractical revolver that he had designed in an effort to evade Colt's patent. And just because the gun was so peculiar the question was raised as to whether or not the patent was valid. There was the likelihood that a court test could have thrown it out, but Smith & Wesson agreed that it would be better business to try to gain exclusive rights to manufacture revolvers with this feature and then hope that other gunmakers would be prevented by the patent from using it. Accordingly, in November 1856 they reached an agreement with Rollin White. White granted

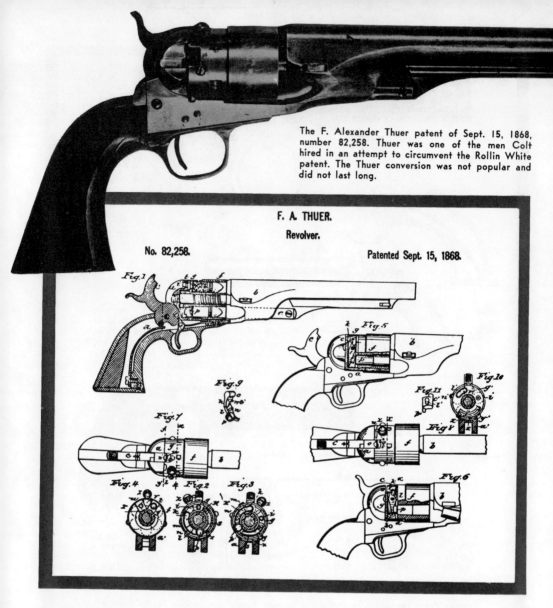

The F. Alexander Thuer patent of Sept. 15, 1868, number 82,258. Thuer was one of the men Colt hired in an attempt to circumvent the Rollin White patent. The Thuer conversion was not popular and did not last long.

F. A. THUER.

Revolver.

No. 82,258.

Patented Sept. 15, 1868.

them this sole right, in return for royalties, while White himself agreed to defend the validity of his patent in the court cases that would ensue. The deal paid off. The patent was attacked, but White and Smith & Wesson came out on top. Until 1869 Smith & Wesson monopolized their field, just as Colt was the leader in the percussion field.

In November 1857 Smith & Wesson at Springfield, Massachusetts began production on their first model .28 caliber seven-shot rimfire which was to become America's first metal cartridge revolver. The cartridge they used was similar to Flobert's

B-B cap rimfire, and it was successful.

The first model S & W, which is without question a superb collector's item for any fancier of early metal cartridge firearms, was a tip-up loading type, .22 caliber rimfire with a rounded brass frame, a two-piece hammer of the hinged-nosed type and a 3⅛″ octagonal barrel. The cylinder catch was located under the lower section of the brass cylinder frame on the earliest and rarest versions. A combination recoil plate and flash shield is incorporated behind the cylinder of the arm which has an overall length of seven inches. Later versions of this fine first model had a flat

D. MOORE.

REVOLVING FIRE-ARM.

No. 187,980.   Patented March 6, 1877.

Fig. 1.

Fig. 5.

Fig. 2.

Fig. 3.

Fig. 4.

Daniel Moore, of Brooklyn, N. Y. Patent number 187,980 dated March 6, 1877. In Moore's own words his invention "consists in so constructing the various parts that by partially rotating the barrel the cylinder is thereby and simultaneously moved longitudinally forward on the axial pin to start the shells from the cylinder."

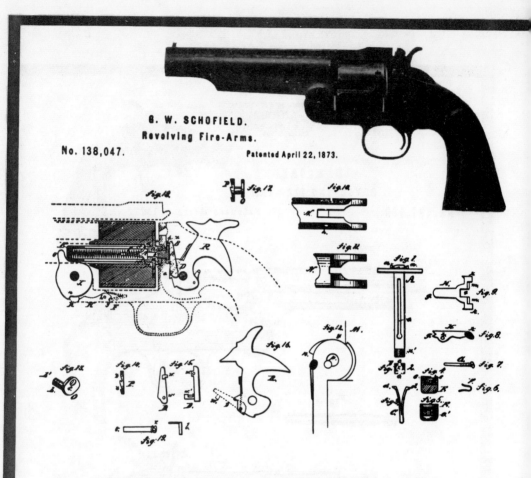

G. W. SCHOFIELD.
Revolving Fire-Arms.

No. 138,047.

Patented April 22, 1873.

George W. Schofield of the United States Army patented number 138,047 on April 22, 1873. This is an unfinished Smith & Wesson revolver with some additions; a 6-inch round barrel with upper rib; caliber .40, 13" overall length, 6-chambered revolving cylinder. Schofield claimed, amongst other items, the combination of an extractor having a hollow or tubular stem and a spring having suitable stops or abutments arranged within the stem.

brass frame and a one-piece hammer. The rifling in the important first model consisted of three left-hand twisting grooves.

Although Smith & Wesson controlled the exclusive rights to the bored-through cylinder and also patented the S & W rimfire cartridge in 1860, their competitors quickly tried to move into the cartridge-loading revolver field and by various dodges to avoid the S & W patents. The percussion cone with its cap was rapidly done away with and cylinders were altered, some by factories themselves and others by independent gunsmiths.

One method used was to cut away a part of the cone end of the cylinder and to replace this with a section welded into place cut from an extra cylinder. The hammer nose was lengthened and the cylinders and barrels were rebored to take a Henry .44 caliber cartridge.

There were a number of faults with the early S & W rimfires. In producing the cartridges the fulminate in the base of the cartridge would frequently not be distributed properly and misfires would result. Also, as in the case of the earlier pin-fire cartridges, cartridges would occasionally be exploded through rough handling. Smith & Wesson, in paying a royalty on

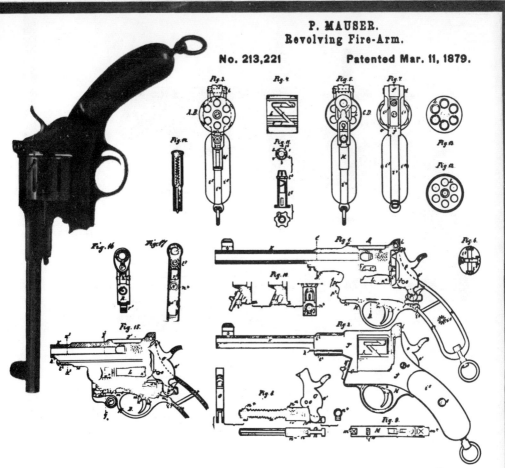

P. MAUSER.
Revolving Fire-Arm.

No. 213,221   Patented Mar. 11, 1879.

Paul Mauser, of Oberndorf, Germany. Patent number 213,221, dated March 11, 1879. The inventor maintained that his revolver could be constructed with only 33 pieces, as against 56 for many other revolvers. To clean the gun a single screw only is unscrewed. Mauser's extractor was also unique.

each weapon turned out with a bored-through cylinder mechanism as part of their contract with Rollin White and insisting that White defend any patent infringements had brought other gunmakers to realize that they had in fact a defensible monopoly. As a result, front-loading cartridge revolvers looked like a possible alternative, for the buyers were eager for the easier handling, quicker loading metal cartridge type revolvers.

Moore's Patent Firearms Company, of Brooklyn, N. Y., produced a caliber .30, six-shot, tit-fire gun, designed to get around the Rollin White patent. This revolver used a metal cartridge which had the priming fulminate contained in a tit-like projection at the base of the cartridge. The cartridge was loaded through the front of the cylinder with the fulminate-contained tit protruding through a hole in the rear of the cylinder. The falling hammer then struck this fulminate tit as it had formerly hit the percussion cap on the cone in the percussion system.

Other manufacturers attempted the front-loading system, including Allen & Wheelock and Bacon. The front-loading system, however, did not hold any more appeal for the buying public than did the

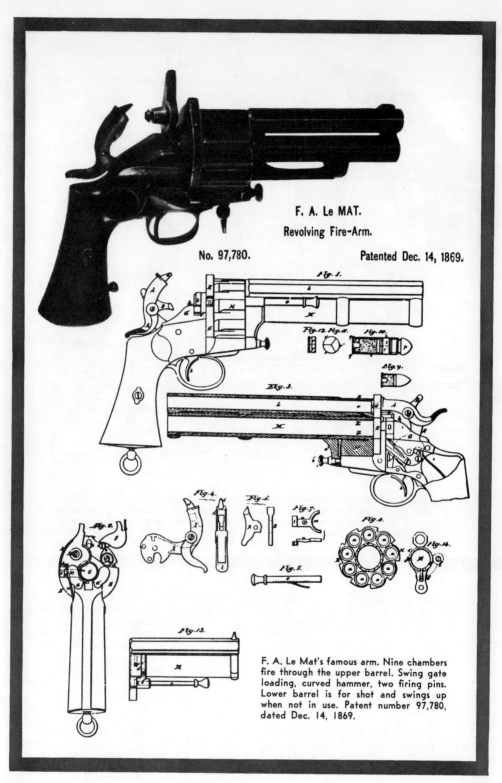

F. A. Le MAT.

Revolving Fire-Arm.

No. 97,780.   Patented Dec. 14, 1869.

F. A. Le Mat's famous arm. Nine chambers fire through the upper barrel. Swing gate loading, curved hammer, two firing pins. Lower barrel is for shot and swings up when not in use. Patent number 97,780, dated Dec. 14, 1869.

idea of crude cylinder conversions, for the best of the frontloaders were makeshift by contrast to the Smith & Wesson rimfires.

Center-fire cartridges, with the fulminate primer located in the middle of the base of the cartridge case, were being experimented with in both England and Germany soon after Flobert designed his rimfire cartridge. Six years after Colt's death, in 1868, the Colt factory tried an unsuccessful alteration to cartridge fire with the F. A. Thuer system. This consisted of loading a rimless center-fire cartridge from the front with a ramming system. The cartridge was tapered so that it seated itself wedge-like at the rear of the cylinder, which had been altered to provide access for the hammer to strike the center of the cartridge base. The system was not commercially successful, and its lack of popularity resulted in few of the Thuer patent conversions of 1868 being marketed.

One weakness of the early Smith & Wessons, besides relatively poor cartridges, was fragility of the weapon's spring-latch-loading breakdown mechanism. In 1869, the year that the Rollin White patent ran out, Wesson was able to correct this flaw by buying patent rights to William Castle Dodge's improved hinge and strengthened spring. That year S & W brought out the "American." The gun was a caliber .44 six-shot single-action Model 1869, the first large caliber Smith & Wesson to be manufactured. Besides the Dodge improvements, the model also included the C. A. King shell extractor. This functioned so that when the top break mechanism was open, a shaft with an extractor rack chamfered into the rear of the cylinder would rise and simultaneously force out the empty shells. The 1869 American also included a trigger guard rather than the sheathed type trigger.

The Smith & Wesson Model of 1875 was a .45 caliber, six-shot single-action, with design changes including a different automatic ejector and a frame-mounted barrel latch, rather than on the barrel, designed by Major George W. Schofield, a cavalry officer. Several slightly different Schofield models were made, but Colt Arms Company was again strongly back in the revolver field and the Schofield model S & W, although a fine weapon, was considered somewhat complicated and never became widely popular. Schofield took his own life with a Schofield in 1882 and his unexpected death canceled exploitation of the gun.

In the West the Smith & Wesson sheathed-trigger, six-shot .32 was highly popular. Although Wild Bill Hickok made his reputation by plugging an armed assailant in the heart at 70 yards with an 1848 Colt percussion Dragoon, and later was known to carry a pair of 1851 model Navy Colts, plus a pair of Derringers and sometimes a rifle, he switched to a cartridge-loading Smith & Wesson.

Yet most of the Western gunmen preferred the single-action Colt '72. This was introduced as a six-shot caliber .45 and in 1878 was rechambered to take the famous Henry .44 or .44-40 Winchester cartridge so popular during that period.

Since many Westerners carried the .44 Winchester rifle, being able to team ammunition with a six-shot revolver was a big selling point. The single-action six shooter of 1872 is uncontested as the most popular revolver ever made. In varying calibers and with slight modifications, it remained in continuous production through 1941.

Colt's first double-action revolver was made in 1877. A small number of these was issued with an oversize jumbo trigger guard. Ostensibly these were for Army use in Alaska so that the gun could be fired by a gloved hand. But this model was also popular in the frontier northwest. Occasionally these rare "carrying-handle" double-action models come to the attention of collectors and are swiftly gobbled up.

About 1875 other leading large-caliber revolver manufacturers included Merwin Hulbert and Company; Hopkins and Allen; Remington, which in 1874 made a caliber .44 Frontier Model, which aside from its sloping frame profile, closely resembled Colt's Model 1872; and Forehand and Wadsworth, all of whom made martial weapons and heavy-duty Western-style six shooters. In sum, the period was one of high action in the firearms field. The inventors did not stagnate; they were not held in check by such things as "virtual monopolies" or problems of accuracy, handling, or maintenance. The greatest ingenuity was brought to bear again and again on those problems that arose with each new step in the progress of firearms; a progress that brought lighter guns, more accurate, with simpler mechanisms, greater power—in short, whatever was required. Where would it eventually lead to? Was there such a thing as a really final and perfect gun? ∎

TOWARD
THE ULTIMATE GUN

What would be the perfect gun? From the time of Roger Bacon until the present there has been the progression of more accurate, powerful and easier-to-handle firearms. How much more could be done? From flintlock to percussion to repeater; and now the magazine. It was lighter, it was streamlined —it functioned swiftly and smoothly with a very minimum of concern from the shooter. Perhaps it, too, can be developed, refined to further perfection.

THERE IS NO record of who invented the first legitimate magazine repeater. Nor do we know where such a weapon was designed. We do know, however, that the famous diarist Samuel Pepys wrote of having seen guns that were repeaters. Some historians have assumed that he referred to two magazine repeaters of that time, the Lorenzoni and the Kalthoff.

The actual name of the inventors of these guns is not known, and so they have been named after a well-known family of gunsmiths who were associated with their early history.

The Kalthoff, developed in the mid-seventeenth century, was a repeater and a magazine gun in the real sense of the word. It had two magazines, as a matter of fact, one for powder, one for balls. The Kalthoff gun was the first magazine repeater to be adopted for military service. Yet, there were weak points in the Kalthoff. It was a delicate weapon and it was also expensive. Because of the precise fitting of parts and the involved system of springs, links, gears, great skill and long hours of work were necessary. And the parts were interdependent. If one thing went wrong, the whole weapon was useless. It was, actually, a weapon for the wealthy or for special troops; not for the average shooter.

The Lorenzoni also had two magazines, one for powder, one for ball. The Lorenzoni was not as safe a gun as the Kalthoff. Because of the rotating breech block there was always the chance of a contact between the powder magazine and breech chamber. For, if the block didn't fit securely, flame could whip back and ignite the powder in the butt. And this actually did happen.

The problem of course was that loading powder and ball separately eliminated the chance of a safe magazine repeater. The answer came in the self-contained metallic cartridge. However, one gun did manage to fill the need before the metallic cartridge appeared on the scene. This was the Winchester rifle.

The Winchester story is loaded with drama and fascinating characters, not the least of whom was Oliver Winchester himself, a former carpenter's apprentice, shirt manufacturer who, it is maintained, knew less about firearms than any man in the business. Indeed, some historians assert that Mr. Winchester never even fired a gun. That, to be sure, is beside the point. His gun was fantastic.

It can be said that the original conception of the Winchester lever-action repeating rifle, Model 1866, the first as a matter of fact to bear the Winchester name, was incorporated in the patents of Walter Hunt's combined piston breech and firing cock repeating gun which he patented August 21, 1849, and in Lewis Jennings' patent of December 25, 1849, for a tubular magazine repeating firearm.

The Hunt and Jennings patents, however, were wrapped in a maze of confusing intercontinental applications. Their patents had been assigned to George Arrowsmith of New York, a machinist. Hunt had first turned his patent over to Arrowsmith; and a highly skilled mechanic in Arrowsmith's shop simplified the Hunt mechanism and obtained an additional patent that same year. This was Lewis Jennings, who in turn released his patent to Arrowsmith. Then Arrowsmith sold the patents to Courtlandt C. Palmer. In 1850, Palmer, a New York financier and one-time president of the Stonington and Providence Railroad, contracted with Robbins & Lawrence of Windsor, Vermont, to manufacture 5000 of the Jennings rifles.

Although these shoulder arms originally had been planned as breechloading repeaters in line with Jennings' patents, the initial production of the models included more simply designed single shot breechloaders as well as the repeaters.

During the period of the Jennings contracts, an inventive machinist, B. Tyler Henry, who was later to play a highly important part in the Winchester development, was an employee of Robbins and Lawrence. Meanwhile Horace Smith, though not associated at this time with Arrowsmith or the others involved in the repeater development, knew that the Jennings multishot was basically a failure, chiefly because the ring trigger which operated the loading mechanism had not functioned efficiently. Smith also learned that B. Tyler Henry had designed an improvement over the ring trigger by replacing it with a lever pivoted at the front of the trigger guard. As the Henry-designed lever was drawn downward, a fresh bullet was forced into the breech at the same time the trigger was automatically cocked. Henry did not have money to patent his development, but he had confided his knowledge of the Jennings rifle, the failure of the original and his improvement to the mechanism, to Smith. Without doubt Henry had spoken to Smith in the hope that he would receive financial backing for a patent application.

Although B. Tyler Henry's name does not appear on any patent papers, a patent issued to Horace Smith of Norwich, Conn.,

H. SMITH & D. B. WESSON.
MAGAZINE FIREARM.

No. 10,535.   Patented Feb. 14, 1854.

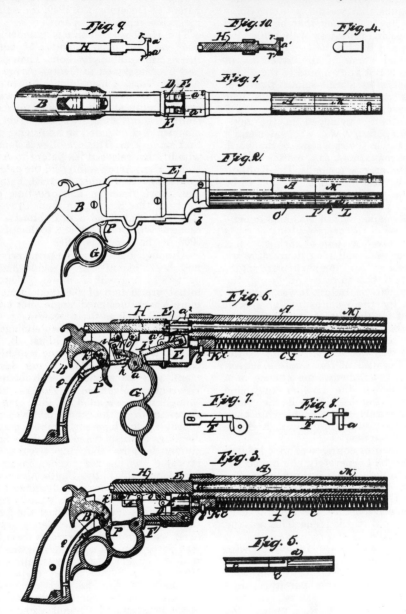

Horace Smith and Daniel B. Wesson, patent number 10,535 dated Feb. 14, 1854. A magazine pistol. Because of the arrangement and application of the percussion hammer, with
respect to the breech-slide and the trigger guard lever, the hammer can be moved and
set to full cock by the pressure or back action of the slide induced by the action of the
trigger guard lever.

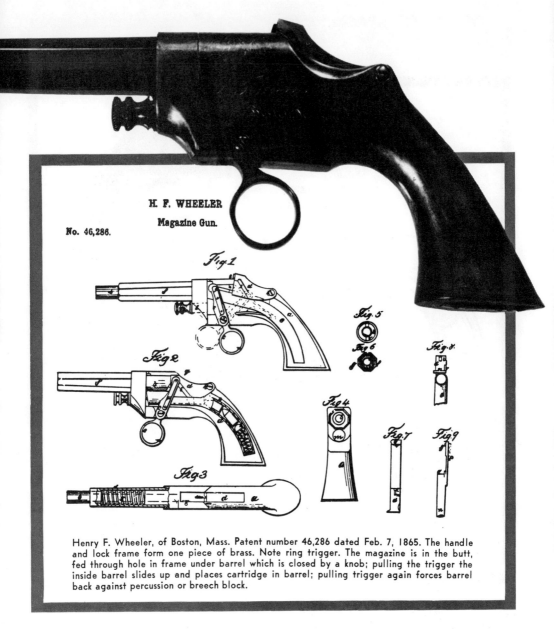

H. F. WHEELER
Magazine Gun.

No. 46,286.

Henry F. Wheeler, of Boston, Mass. Patent number 46,286 dated Feb. 7, 1865. The handle and lock frame form one piece of brass. Note ring trigger. The magazine is in the butt, fed through hole in frame under barrel which is closed by a knob; pulling the trigger the inside barrel slides up and places cartridge in barrel; pulling trigger again forces barrel back against percussion or breech block.

August 26, 1851, concerned an improvement on the Jennings patent of 1849, and undoubtedly was a result of Henry's ingenuity.

Throughout Henry's relationship with Smith & Wesson his name did not appear in any of the patent applications, although in 1854 Smith took out another patent of some importance in the line of progress toward the initial Winchester 1866, and

Henry is thought to have been its originator too.

This 1854 Smith patent was for a metallic-type cartridge including internal ignition by means of a "disk resting directly on the primer with the priming in the rear of the disk." During the next two years Smith & Wesson concentrated their efforts on repeating rifles and pistols, making use of the Hunt-type loaded ball ammunition

101

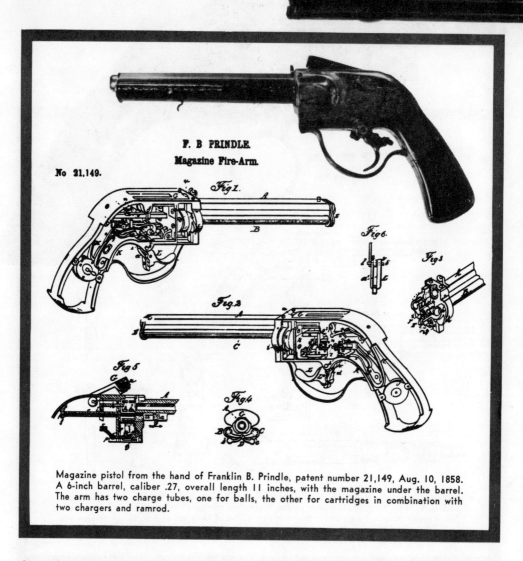

F. B PRINDLE.
Magazine Fire-Arm.

No 21,149.

Fig 1.

Fig 2.

Fig 3.

Fig 4.

Fig 5.

Fig 6.

Fig 8.

Magazine pistol from the hand of Franklin B. Prindle, patent number 21,149, Aug. 10, 1858. A 6-inch barrel, caliber .27, overall length 11 inches, with the magazine under the barrel. The arm has two charge tubes, one for balls, the other for cartridges in combination with two chargers and ramrod.

plus a lever action and under-the-barrel tubular magazine. The arms were loaded through a cutout near the forward end of the spring equipped magazine tube. The bullets, which were cylindro-conoidal in shape, had blunt tips to prevent accidental firing of adjacent cartridges.

The repeating pistols held eight to ten cartridges each and the rifles twenty shots. They were made in three calibers, .31, .36, .44 according to S & W records. In spite of the blunt tipped cartridges, the Smith &

Wesson repeaters, like other repeaters of the era, had the unfortunate habit of chain firing, although the danger of chain ignition was somewhat less in the S & W tubular repeater than in the early percussion revolvers and revolving rifles.

One of the big weaknesses of the Smith & Wesson tubular repeating arms was the corrosive effect caused by the fulminate of mercury used in the cartridges. Although the same corrosive effect occurred in muzzle-loaders, these could be

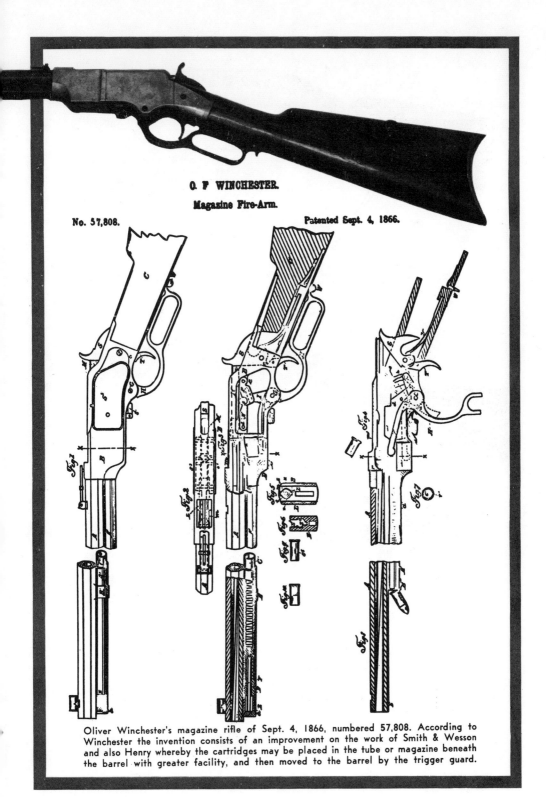

O. F. WINCHESTER.

Magazine Fire-Arm.

No. 57,808.   Patented Sept. 4, 1866.

Oliver Winchester's magazine rifle of Sept. 4, 1866, numbered 57,808. According to Winchester the invention consists of an improvement on the work of Smith & Wesson and also Henry whereby the cartridges may be placed in the tube or magazine beneath the barrel with greater facility, and then moved to the barrel by the trigger guard.

Christian W. Buchel of New York, N.Y.,
patent number 6,136 dated Feb. 20,
1849. The gun has a long brass magazine tube, and a long lever on the
right side of the lock plate that operates the piston plunger.

C. W. BUCHEL.
Magazine Fire-arm.

No. 6,136.

Patented Feb. 20, 1849.

B. B. HOTCHKISS.
MAGAZINE FIRE-ARMS.

No. 184,285.

Patented Nov. 14, 1876

Fig:1.

Fig:6.   **Fig:5.**

The Benjamin B. Hotchkiss gun has a
bolt lock, an open front sight, and an
elevating rear sight. The arm can be
used either as a single breechloader
or as a magazine arm. Patent number
184,285; November 14, 1876.

Fig:2.   **Fig:4.**   **Fig:7.**   **Fig:3.**

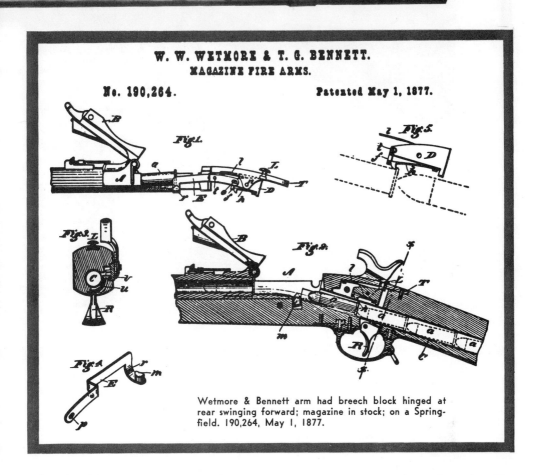

W. W. WETMORE & T. G. BENNETT.
MAGAZINE FIRE ARMS.

No. 190,264.   Patented May 1, 1877.

Wetmore & Bennett arm had breech block hinged at rear swinging forward; magazine in stock; on a Springfield. 190,264, May 1, 1877.

rebored and larger ammunition used. However, the ammunition in the Smith & Wessons was limited to the inner diameter of the tubular magazine, so as soon as the grooves and lands in the Smith & Wesson arms became excessively worn, there was nothing to do but replace the barrel.

In August 1855 all of the tools, machinery, models and completed parts of pistols left over from an estimated 1200 which were manufactured during Smith & Wesson's limited partnership with Courtlandt Palmer were moved to Orange street in New Haven. Wesson moved with the new Volcanic Company and worked briefly as its superintendent. Henry went back to his old job with Robbins and Lawrence. In 1856 Wesson left Volcanic to work with Smith on the Rollin White idea. The Volcanic Repeating Firearms Company was left without a single man amongst the stockholders who had the least experience with firearms. But Oliver Winchester was a shrewd individual and he hired William C. Hicks away from Colt to take over direction of the company. In 1857 Volcanic Arms was declared insolvent, and by court order the entire assets of the defunct company were assigned to Winchester who was the firm's principal creditor.

Even before Volcanic had gone into final receivership Winchester had formed the New Haven Arms Company. He chose B. Tyler Henry as plant superintendent. By 1861 the New Haven was in financial diffi-

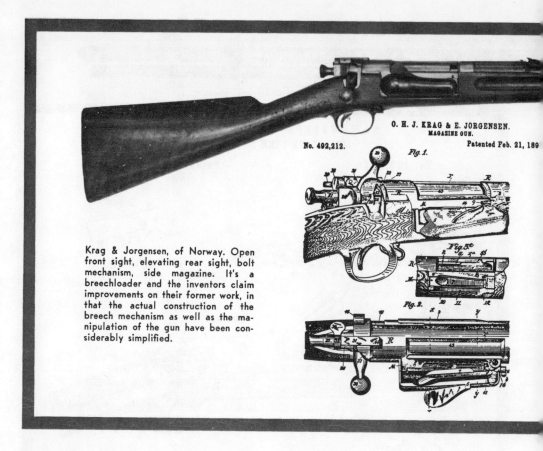

O. H. J. KRAG & E. JORGENSEN.
MAGAZINE GUN.

No. 492,212.

Patented Feb. 21, 189

Fig. 1.

Fig. 5

Fig. 2.

Krag & Jorgensen, of Norway. Open front sight, elevating rear sight, bolt mechanism, side magazine. It's a breechloader and the inventors claim improvements on their former work, in that the actual construction of the breech mechanism as well as the manipulation of the gun have been considerably simplified.

culties. The Volcanic, it appears, lacked only proper ammunition to become a popular weapon.

By the end of 1858 B. Tyler Henry had developed a flange-type rimfire cartridge which had an annular recess around the rim in which fulminating powder was placed. The cartridges had conically shaped 216 grain bullets with a powder charge of about 25 to 30 grains. Later the bullet was changed to flat nose, the base was marked with an H and the cartridges were termed the Henry .44 flats. These .44s developed a muzzle velocity of 1200′ per second as contrasted to the 500′ per second of the original Volcanic ammunition.

The Volcanic repeating mechanism was then altered and modified to handle the new ammunition. These modifications primarily concerned a split type firing pin which struck two sides of the curled over fulminate charged lip, vastly reducing the possibility of misfire, and modifying the gun to extract the rimfire type cartridges.

The .44 caliber ammunition, considerably larger than the Volcanic's .393″ bore,

was doubtless an attempt to gain military adoption and was the heaviest caliber practical to the construction of the gun though still considerably smaller than the standard military caliber .50.

The redesigned arm was patented in 1800 in Henry's name. The new gun called the Henry's Patent Repeating Rifle proved to be the turning point for the New Haven Arms Company. Oliver Winchester presently changed the title of the new company to the Winchester Repeating Arms Company. The first firearm to be produced by the new company was the Model 1866, the first gun to bear the Winchester name. The loading and firing mechanism varied from the Henry only with an improved cartridge extractor. The ammunition was rimfire, much the same as used in the Henry, though the powder load was increased from 25 to 28 grains and the bullet was reduced from 216 to 200 grains.

The chief modification of the '66, as it was called, from the Henry was in the magazine and its loading arrangement. The cartridges were inserted directly into the

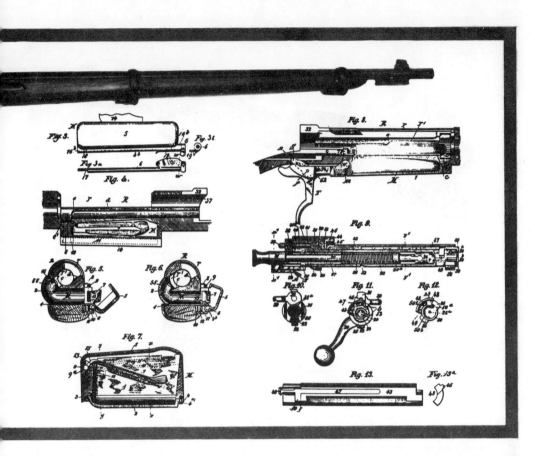

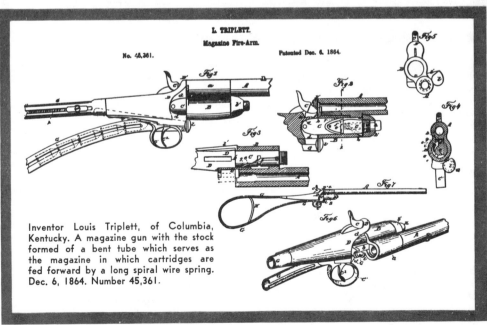

L. TRIPLETT.
Magazine Fire-Arm.

No. 45,361.

Patented Dec. 6. 1864.

Inventor Louis Triplett, of Columbia, Kentucky. A magazine gun with the stock formed of a bent tube which serves as the magazine in which cartridges are fed forward by a long spiral wire spring. Dec. 6, 1864. Number 45,361.

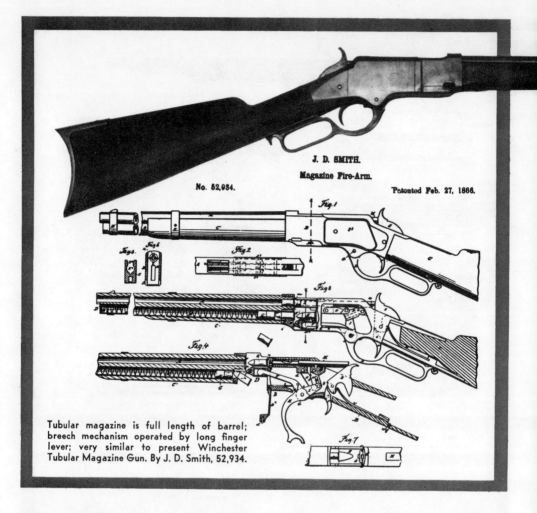

J. D. SMITH.
Magazine Fire-Arm.

No. 52,934.

Patented Feb. 27, 1866.

Fig.1

Fig.2

Fig.4

Fig.5
Fig.6

Fig.3

Fig.7

Tubular magazine is full length of barrel; breech mechanism operated by long finger lever; very similar to present Winchester Tubular Magazine Gun. By J. D. Smith, 52,934.

front portion of the Henry magazine. The Model '66 had a spring cover on the right side of the receiver and cartridges were loaded by pushing down this cover.

Although the rifle became known as a fifteen or sixteen shot repeater, in rifle or musket form it had a capacity of seventeen cartridges and as a carbine, thirteen cartridges.

Now the Henry rifle was dropped and full work went into the '66. Later the Model 1873 was introduced. It was produced in .44 caliber only until 1879 when a .38-40 center-fire chambering was added. The '73 rifles had a capacity of fifteen cartridges in standard version or six cartridges in short, tubular magazine version.

We have mentioned the fabulous Christopher M. Spencer and his repeating rifle in a previous chapter. It was Spencer who was really the first to bring out a repeater,

seven months before the Henry. The Spencer was patented March 6, 1860. It was not self-cocking, as the Henry was; the hammer had to be drawn back for each shot by hand. Also, it held less than half the shots the Henry did. At the same time, it was a sturdier gun, simpler in construction, and moreover, cheaper. It had lever action, pumping cartridges from a tubular magazine in the butt into the chamber; then it ejected them after firing.

When the Spencer company failed in 1869 all its assets were put to auction. The biggest buyer was Oliver Winchester. Indeed, it may be said that Winchester's winning the western market had ruined Spencer. Winchester was now without any serious rival.

Even while the Civil War was still in progress European designers were busy studying bolt action as against lever action

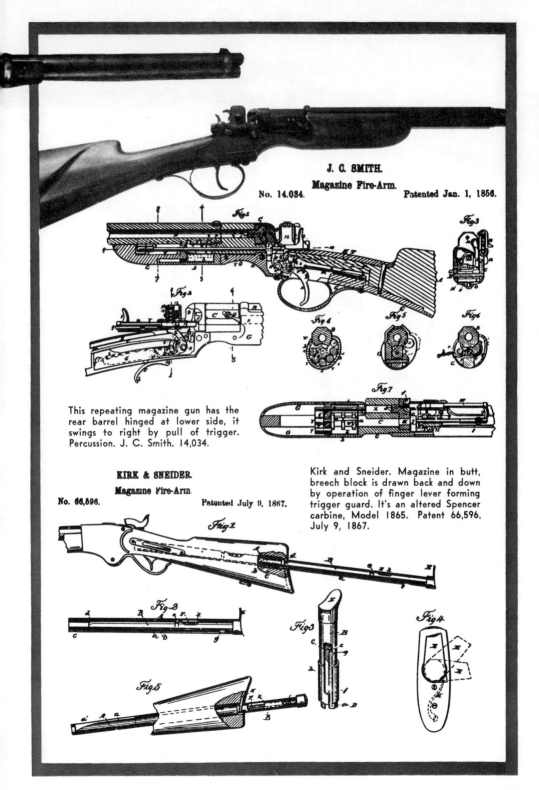

J. C. SMITH.
Magazine Fire-Arm.

No. 14,034. Patented Jan. 1, 1856.

This repeating magazine gun has the rear barrel hinged at lower side, it swings to right by pull of trigger. Percussion. J. C. Smith. 14,034.

KIRK & SNEIDER
Magazine Fire-Arm.

No. 66,596. Patented July 9, 1867.

Kirk and Sneider. Magazine in butt, breech block is drawn back and down by operation of finger lever forming trigger guard. It's an altered Spencer carbine, Model 1865. Patent 66,596, July 9, 1867.

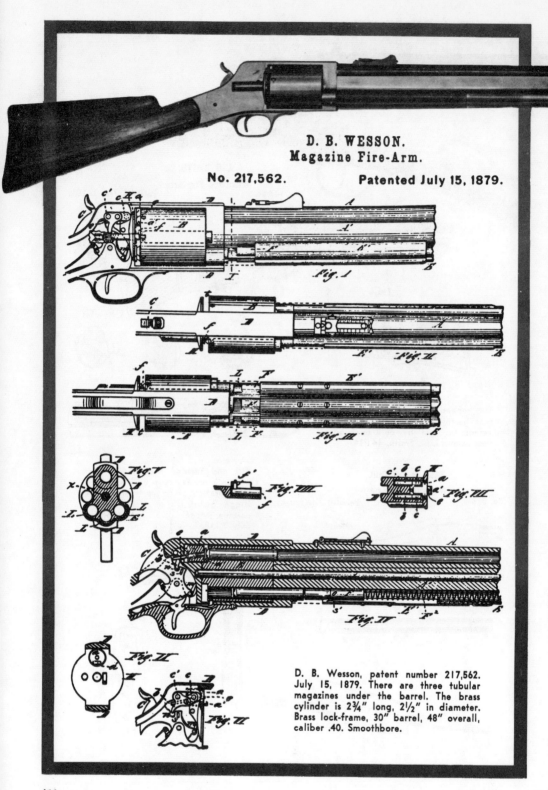

D. B. WESSON.
Magazine Fire-Arm.

No. 217,562.   **Patented July 15, 1879.**

Fig. 1

Fig. II

Fig. III

Fig. V   *Fig. VIII*   *Fig. VII*

Fig. IV

Fig. VI   *Fig. VI*

D. B. Wesson, patent number 217,562.
July 15, 1879. There are three tubular
magazines under the barrel. The brass
cylinder is 2¾" long, 2½" in diameter.
Brass lock-frame, 30" barrel, 48" overall,
caliber .40. Smoothbore.

for the repeating rifle. In Switzerland Frederick Vetterli developed a bolt action rifle with a tubular magazine beneath the barrel; and in Germany Peter Paul Mauser brought the bolt action to the acme of perfection for metallic cartridge arms. In America bolt action repeaters with Spencer-type tube magazines in the stock appeared. The Hotchkiss and the Chaffee-Reese were notable.

These arms were steps on the ladder of progress. James P. Lee, a Scotsman who became a United States citizen designed a box magazine that was directly below the bolt. In 1879 it was adopted for Navy use, and in a short while it was used all over the world.

The idea of the loading clip had been in the minds of some inventors for a long time. It appeared to be the next step that would bring the repeater to its proper stat-

ure. Sam Colt had had the idea, using extra cylinders for some of his revolvers, and so had Christopher Spencer. The idea of the box magazine was seized upon eagerly by Ferdinand von Mannlicher, the Austrian. Mannlicher was a true genius, and some of his ideas were years ahead of his time. Nearly all of the clips that are in use today are variations of Mannlicher's work.

We have been able to describe and show pictures of only a small amount of the fascinating items that are at the Smithsonian. There is no doubt that this collection is amongst the finest in the world. Here is a rich deposit, a true eldorado for the student or the expert who wants to know more about the development of guns not only in the United States but in the world. The story is all there; where it will lead to from here is another question.

One can say that the magazine repeater is now fully developed. Is the gun perfect? Assuredly there will be refinements, adaptations. Inventors will still invent and their products will still move the world. The firearms story is not ended. In a sense, it may just be starting on something new, something none of us can yet envision.

In any event, we know for certain that nothing remains at a standstill, and the progress of the gun is no exception.

Lewis Jennings' breechloading magazine gun is pill lock with tubular magazine, 34" barrel, 53" overall, caliber .50. Dated Dec. 25, 1849, number 6,973. In combination with the magazine for containing cartridges or loaded balls, which communicates with the barrel, there is a sliding charger for the purpose of forcing the cartridges toward the rear of the magazine.